Poetry
for
Animals

Also by I. H. Smythe

Stories for Animals
Dwynwen's Feast

I. H. SMYTHE

Poetry for Animals

Illustrated by
Sappho

iUniverse, Inc.
Bloomington

Poetry for Animals

Copyright © 2011 I. H. Smythe

iUniverse books may be ordered through booksellers or by contacting:

iUniverse
1663 Liberty Drive
Bloomington, IN 47403
www.iuniverse.com
1-800-Authors (1-800-288-4677)

ISBN: 978-1-4620-0199-6 (pbk)
ISBN: 978-1-4620-0201-6 (cloth)
ISBN: 978-1-4620-0200-9 (ebk)

Printed in the United States of America

iUniverse rev. date: 2/18/2011

To Rigel, Sappho, and Steve,
who believed in my ability
to rhyme every word in the English language
with every other word.
Because of your faith in me
I can now rhyme
turtle with fire hydrant.
Thank you.

If you are reading this, you are an animal.

Maybe you should get off the furniture.

Contents

Preface

Dear Reader:

You may well be wondering why this book of poetry is specifically for animals. It is because, sadly, my books *Poetry for Potatoes, More Poetry for Potatoes,* and even my multivolume set entitled *Even More Poetry for Potatoes Damn and Blast It* have not done at all well in the marketplace (I blame the economy) and I have learned from my mistakes. Of course all poetry is for animals really, which you will discover if you recite a poem to a cloud, a fungus, or some office furniture. They're generally not very interested, and you will probably find that the cloud will just drift away, the fungus will slowly rot, and the office furniture will look bored and expressionless. Animals, on the other hand, are usually very interested in poetry, although you have to pick your animal and pick your moment, of course. I wouldn't attempt to recite a Shakespearean sonnet, for example, to a bear who is chasing you through the woods, even though the woods are an ideal setting for a poetry recitation. This is because no bear in all of history has ever thought to itself, "Because I am hearing such beautiful poetry I will not eat this tasty young person." Poetry is not an appetite suppressant, unless it is a poem about earwax, projectile vomiting, or the billions of micro-organisms that live and breed on your food. Clearly the diet industry would do well to employ more poets, and possibly more bears in order to provide their clients with a compelling reason to exercise.

But I digress. Animals *do* enjoy poetry, but the animals who enjoy poetry most are the great apes, and among these Homo sapiens are the clear winners. It is we humans who have learned to write and to enjoy both kinds of poetry. By the way, you may be thinking that the two kinds of poetry are poems that rhyme and poems that don't but, especially if you are a child, you will agree with me that poems that don't rhyme aren't really poems at all. (Note that the classic work entitled *A Children's Book of Blank Verse* does not exist.) This is because when you are a child and your mother reads to you at bedtime, if she tells you that she is going to read a poem, you know that you will hear rhyming words – every single time. If there are no rhyming words, then you know that your mother has chosen something else for your bedtime reading, such as a story, a shopping list, a prescription, a diary excerpt, or a ransom note.

(Incidentally, in order to challenge myself, I often write my diary excerpts, ransom notes, and grocery lists in rhyme, which is much trickier than it sounds. Take grocery lists: if I want jam, for instance, the only other things I can buy are ham, clam, lamb, and Spam because these are the only foods that rhyme with jam. And because I am a vegetarian, this puts me in rather a pickle – another food I can't buy, because the only things that rhyme with pickle are nickel and sickle and, call me fickle, but I don't eat coins or farming implements either.)

No, the two different kinds of poems are long poems and short poems, and you'll be pleased to know that I have mastered both varieties. The definition of a short poem is one that takes under two minutes to read, whereas a long poem can keep going for decades and only ends when you plummet headlong into your grave. (Some people prefer to have long poems read *to* them so that they can lie down with their eyes closed and their arms crossed over their chests – just in case.)

In this volume of poetry for animals you will find that the long poems, and even some of the short ones, have helpful study guides or questions after them. Do not be alarmed! Unlike most study guides, these are not meant to terrify and confuse, until the young reader starts slavering like a mad dog and gnawing bits out of Teacher's leg. (You know what I mean – surely you've had the experience of coming to the end of a poem about, say, a girl and her unicorn, only to be asked the question, "How did the author use the unicorn as a metaphor?" when all the time you thought the unicorn was used as a form of transportation.) No, the study guides included in this volume are meant both to spare Teacher's leg, and also to provide ever greater opportunities for pleasure and happiness.

It is my sincere hope that you will enjoy these poems for animals, my animal friend, and that they might inspire you to take up pen and paper, chalk and blackboard, even stick and sandbox, and write some poems of your own.

Most sincerely,

I. H. Smythe

PS: And just in case you were wondering –
Besides poems
Both short and long,
I have also mastered free verse –
As is evident
From this paragraph.

PPS: And like my book *Stories for Animals,* this book was written with the students of Westmount Charter School in mind, all of whom have terrifyingly huge brains though, thankfully, not terrifyingly huge heads.

The Lizard

Young Stanley was the sort of boy
That you would never guess,
Would get himself, his mom, the Earth,
In any sort of mess.
He said his prayers, he combed his hairs,
His room was span-and-spic.
He'd shovel snow, the lawn he'd mow,
He never once was sick.
He'd always clean his plate, preferring broccoli to sweets.
He gave alms to the poor
Whilst helping nuns across the streets.
In all his ways and deeds he shone – "angelic" is the word,
In math, in death, in lunch, in life,
Young Stanley never erred.
And into beastly mischief Stanley seldom was enticed,
How strange, then, that he's now known
As the Little Antichrist,
And all because the *once* he was a slightly naughty boy,
Who spent his pocket money on a plastic, packaged toy
Instead of butter, which his Mother'd sent him out to get,
For evermore (so not that long)
A choice Stan would regret.

The trouble started when young Stan
Went to the store to buy
The butter, but instead another item caught his eye.

He laid his eyes, then laid his hands,
Then laid his butter bills
Upon the counter, for a lizard,
Green, with thorns and frills,
And two-pronged tongue and flaming eyes
That bulged as big as quarters,
("No mere child could fight its charms!"
He later told reporters.)
Its tiny size, its bloodshot eyes, and overpowering smell,
Convinced him it would be a hit
At next day's show and tell,
So slipping *both* the butter and the lizard in his pocket,
He bolted from the crime scene
Like his pants contained a rocket.
Arriving home young Stanley put away the booty butter;
"I'll be upstairs with . . . nothing . . ."
His poor mother heard him mutter.
And with a flashlight, under cover, in his trundle bed,
He emptied out his pockets
And then from the package read:

> Welcome you to growing pet,
> he you will be surprising,
> Now dream of lizard-owning
> happy joy you realizing!
> This funny strangely toy
> extend ten times familiar size,

When please exposed to children
it increasing for your eyes.
For best enjoyment texture
slimy icky please you liking,
But beware *chung yung fu fat fung,*
or woeful fengshui striking.
And insert not in children
or to doctor have a chat,
He happy not a source of
transubstantiated fat!

With this young Stanley opened up
The package and withdrew
The lizard – and his love, just like the lizard,
Grew and grew.
And by the time he fell asleep that night upon his bed,
That lizard was much bigger than a box for holding bread.
Its shape was roughly lizoid, like a huge Komodo dragon,
But massive, like a thing that you would climb
And stick a flag in.
And when he woke next morning
What did Stanley find was there?
A twenty-five ton lizard where there normally was air!
It crushed him to his mattress!
Stanley couldn't breathe for slime!
But he slithered out his second-story window just in time,
And fell *kersplat* in lizard gunk, in green reptilian flows,

Exuding out the windows like some mucus from a nose.
And Stanley had to claw his way
Through oozing, greenish goop,
Like something just emerging
From that first primordial soup,
And creeping free he ran to tell his mom,
But then he thought, if he
Told her, then for that one buttered crime
He would be caught.
And so he went to school attired in jammies most informal,
And hoped his mother wouldn't notice anything abnormal.

That day was long for Stanley
Since he stank like rotting trout,
And his schoolmates held their noses,
And a few of them passed out.
At show and tell time Stanley was unnerved
But kept his head,
Since he didn't have his toy,
He shew and told his pants instead.
With eloquence, like it was planned,
He spoke of jammie britches,
With waistband of elastic
And with hems of running stitches.
He spoke of washing labels
And of stripes of white and brown,
And showed how he could pull them up,

And then could pull them down . . .
And showed that even if you're in pyjamas you can stand,
In a corner – with a dunce cap – at Teacher's command.
But finally the home-bell rang and leaping from their seats,
They flowed like bubbling liquid
Out the doors into the streets,
All so relieved to get away from Stanley and his stench,
Because he stank like *merde* in the *sol,* excuse my French.
And as for Stan he shuffled home,
Afraid he'd be in trouble,
For possibly reducing hearth and home to rock and rubble,
For wearing jammies, skipping breakfast,
Smelling kind of weird,
But these were just the least of all the things
He should have feared . . .
He *should* have been afraid,
Because he'd surely had some warning,
His house might well expand
And then explode that very morning,
His lizard might keep growing giving everyone a shock,
Crushing cars and houses flat within a city block.
He *should* have feared that by his lizard
Folks would be molested,
And that in only moments he was going to be arrested.
And that the press would shortly shove
Their mikes into his face,
And that it all would end in tears and permanent disgrace.

He *should* have feared it since, in fact,
It happened in this way,
The headlines read:
Boy, 10, Wrecks House, Mom Grounds Him For One Day.
And well he knew that "mischief"
Shouldn't be the only charge,
The headlines read:
Some Butter Stolen, Culprit Still At Large!

Oh foolish boy! If only Stan had been a little quicker,
To see and peel off from the box
The *Made In China* sticker!
For underneath the sticker on the lizard's plastic wrap,
Were words that clearly showed
This little toy was just a trap!
The package claimed the beast would grow
"Ten times familiar size,"
But obviously such a claim was just a pack of lies!
The truth below the sticker
Might have stopped this foul T-rex,
Because it read, as plain as day,
"Ten times . . . a *googolplex*!"
Quite possibly the scariest of numbers e'er invented,
Without which this catastrophe
Might well have been prevented!
But no! Too late! Police and soldiers
Found their efforts crippled,

By the fact that, every hour, the lizard's size was tripled!
They tried to stop it growing and secreting vile jelly,
They dropped atomic bombs
While all the children kicked its belly!
They set the thing aflame
While on it fireworks were dumped,
But on it grew till every herpetologist was stumped!
And so were SWAT teams, so were ninjas,
Psychics, gurus, vets,
And motivational speakers who like motivating pets,
And lawyers who had tried to stop the lizard with a law,
Which didn't work, so people stuffed
The lawyers in its maw!
But still it thrashed and crushed and bashed
While from it sewage squirted,
Till true believers lost their faith
And atheists converted!
And so it wasn't long till the community was choked –
The headlines read:
Boy, 10, Wrecks Town, Allowance Is Revoked.
And soon the number of the towns he'd wrecked
Surpassed a million!
The headlines read:
Boy, 10, Wrecks Earth, Age 4.54 billion.
And so on till the Truth appeared in headlines that all said:
Butter Thief, 10, Wrecks the Cosmos, Everybody Dead!

What happened next? I'm sure that you
Don't need the details filled in,
Remember what the package said
When "please exposed to children."
But since the children met their doom
It's really no surprise,
The hateful lizard dwindled till it reached its normal size.
And there it sat upon the Earth dejected and forlorn,
Till history began again and you, of course, were born.
And now it waits upon a shelf for someone else to buy it,
It waits to turn another kid into a butter-pirate,
And thence into a scapegoat as it grows and squirts its goo,
The question is, I wonder – will that someone else be you?

Study Guide

1. The label on the lizard's package says, *"Chung yung fu fat fung"* which is obviously a warning of some kind, written in Chinese. Do you think these are real Chinese words, or did the author just make something up because she was too lazy to do any research? If they are made-up words, do you believe that in the age of the Internet this sort of inattention to detail can be forgiven? Do you believe it makes it funnier if the words are made-up, or has the author accidentally insulted about a billion people and should probably leave the country until things cool down a little?

2. Regardless of whether or not the words are made-up, what do you think the warning is? Do you think a simple warning is enough, or should infinitely-expanding lizards be outlawed? Do you believe that such a ban would infringe on your basic human right to own whatever you want to own, even if it is a danger to other people? If you agree that it does infringe on your individual rights, should you also be allowed to own a large dog who eats only anthrax-and-razorblade kibble and will explode on command? What about a nuclear powered tsunami generator or an active, portable volcano? Should you be allowed to own and operate a killer bee circus? If you have a secret lab, should you be allowed to stitch

together a killer whale, a malaria-carrying mosquito, and a box jellyfish into one hideous monstrosity, and then bring it to Bring-Your-Pet-To-School Day? Do you believe that your teacher would think this was entirely reasonable as long as the other students were armed with nunchucks in order to defend themselves?

The question is where do you, personally, draw the line? Do you think that *you* should be allowed to own dangerous things but other people shouldn't? Do these other people include your brother or sister? Elaborate and defend your position with a poison dart frog or avalanche gun if necessary.

3. In the course of your childhood adventures, have you yourself ever almost accidentally destroyed the Earth? Were you punished for this or are your parents both mad scientists who intend to conquer the globe and use it for their own sinister purposes, and so they patted you on the head and took you out for ice cream?

4. You may be wondering what a scapegoat is and why it's a goat at all and not, say, a skate or a snake. (Of course, the likely reason is because a person can't say scapesnake or scapeskate really fast even just twice without stumbling, and people in ancient times, who already dressed and talked funny, were sensitive about looking even dumber.) A scapegoat used to be an actual real live

goat that got blamed for everything – like Mr. Nobody, except that he doesn't eat the labels off tin cans and bleat. In olden times, if you sinned by breaking your mother's best china serving dish, or stole millions of dollars off people through corrupt business practices, it was perfectly acceptable to just blame the goat and let him get in trouble instead of you. "The goat did it" was probably a very popular phrase and eventually, after the goat had done enough, the people would drive it off into the wilderness so they wouldn't have to think about all the broken dishes and Ponzi schemes that had gone so horribly wrong.

Nowadays, a scapegoat is a person who gets blamed for everything even though it isn't that person's fault, and here you know I'm talking about you and that time in class when – well, there's no reason to rehash all the ugly details here. The point is that scapegoating is very wrong and that blaming a goat for stealing millions of dollars from people is also extremely silly. I say blame goats for stealing millions of dollars from people only if they've actually done it. Then you can drive them into the wilderness if you like, but at least they'll be able to afford a nice limousine and a chauffeur.

5. What are alms and why do needy people seem to like them so much? Do you feel that you, personally, are needy? If so, do you intend to ask for alms for your

birthday?

6. "The Lizard" contains an extremely naughty word in the French language, which explains why this poem has probably been banned from your school and if your mother knew you were reading this she would snatch it away and make you pray for forgiveness. What do you think this word is? If you already know what it is, do you intend to say it the next time you stub your toe, or will you rely on one of your old standbys? Do you think saying bad words in other languages makes you appear more worldly and sophisticated? If you say a bad word in another language, are you afraid that someone who actually speaks that language will overhear you and then, believing that you are a fluent speaker, ask you for directions to a complicated location? If this happens, do you intend to mime the pretend-fact that you are deaf in order to avoid embarrassment? If you actually are deaf, do you intend to use sign language to say this word, thereby shocking two language-speaking-communities at once?

7. When was the last time you yourself helped a nun across a street? Are you ashamed of your track record in the nun-helping department, or have you helped enough bishops across the street to make up for it?

8. You may be wondering who the Antichrist is (and if there is an Antichrist, is there also an Unclechrist, to which the answer is, "Maybe it's time you had a little talk with your uncle"). The Antichrist is, essentially, the bad guy – think of Voldemort or Count Olaf, in a bad mood, having a bad hair day, and then multiply that level of badness by a googolplex (as in this formula:

Vmort + CountO × googolplex = AntiC

– a formula with which you can now impress your math teacher, if your math teacher happens to have an IQ under 75). That's how bad the Antichrist is; he's the type who never helps nuns across streets but deliberately pushes them in front of moving vehicles while swearing in French and trying to bring about the end of civilization as we know it. He's the type of supernatural being who wants everyone to be dead and suffering in the fires of hell, rather than alive and playing computer games or watching TV. If I were you I would avoid the Antichrist; he likes plagues and famines and you wouldn't have anything in common, trust me. So if your mother feels sorry for him because she thinks he's just unloved and insists on inviting him to your next birthday party, I would suggest you make your position clear by throwing a good old-fashioned, full-blown temper tantrum, like the kind you used to throw in the aisles of grocery stores when you were little, if you didn't like which way the wind was blowing. Tell her that he hates ice cream and party games and will probably try to kill everybody. If she still insists on inviting him, make sure you keep the cake-cutting knife out of reach, pretend you're glad he broke all your presents, and make somebody else be his partner in the three-legged race.

9. In the preceding poem, the author wrote that the lizard's slime exuded "out the windows like some mucus from a nose." In your opinion which is funnier: the word "mucus" or the word "snot?" Did the author miss a golden opportunity by not writing, "Exuding out the window like some *snot* from someone's nose?" Conduct a scientific experiment by whipping the word "snot" on a wide range of people (a baby, the Pope, your teacher) and chart the results.

10. How did you answer the question in the final line of the poem? If you answered *yes,* do you now feel it is your destiny to be the next person who buys the dreaded growing lizard, and so you can never be truly happy ever again? If you answered *no,* is this because you intend to wear your fingers to bloody stumps by peeling off the *Made in China* labels from products before you buy them so you can never be fooled? Discuss and lay blame.

Little Love 'ems

Gentle Kitty on my pillow,
Soft as little pussy willow,
Kitty purring, baby cooing,
Faith in rainbows now renewing.
Washing whiskers, one, two, three,
Charming baby, cheering me.

Little Lambie in the bed,
Fluffy as a loaf of bread,
Lambie prancing, baby clapping,
Milk from saucer Lambie's lapping.
Lollipops are not as sweet
As little Lambie's precious bleat.

Darling Bunny on the rug,
Dearest Baby needs a hug,
Bunny nestles, Baby cuddles,
Falls asleep in blanket puddles.
Angels sweet with halos round,
But what's that funny panting sound?

Komodo Dragon rings the bell,
Scary as a fiend from hell,
Dragon growling, neighbours screaming,
Foul breath and nostrils steaming.
"Dragon, I think you could maybe
Spare me, please, and eat the baby."

Know, Know, Know!

It was in class the other day
I heard an ignoramus say,
"I'll never need to know this stuff!
Learning's dumb – I've had enough."
He then kicked Teacher in the knee,
And on his books he took a wee,
Then fled to safety and TV.
Oh foolish boy! So thick! So slow!
He doesn't know he doesn't know,
He's unaware he's unaware,
Of what he'll need to know somewhere
Someday, when faced with perils great,
What will save him from his fate,
Will be what he has learned – too late!

Take the case of Babs McLilty,
(Names are changed to protect the guilty),
Who, when told, "Learn seven times eight,"
Didn't – thus did her doom await.
For when her parents took her away
To a savage land – on holiday –
(Where studying is only prudent,
Since teachers live on boiled student)
The girl was snatched, tied to a chair,
A dunce cap placed upon her hair,

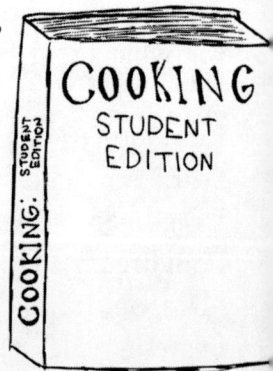

And 'round her danced the sadists mad,
Insisting she subtract and add.
Her parents, who were sipping tea,
And lunching on biscuits and brie,
Were unconcerned; they knew their daughter,
Though she faced imminent slaughter,
Went to a school for girls elite,
And so they yawned, and turned to Cheat.
The savages continued taunting,
But Babs gave them what they were wanting.
They aimed their bows, screamed, "Four plus seven!"
Babs rolled her eyes, and said "eleven."
And only once she answered, "Um . . ."
But quickly came up with the sum.
For all the easy ones she knew,
And hard ones, like, "one minus two."
And on it went, until a brute
Screamed, "Multiply! Or else we'll shoot!"
And Babs looked bored, composed, sedate,
Until she heard, "Seven times eight."
And then the sweat began to pour,
And addled Babs said, "Fifty-four?"
The savages took aim and smiled.
Her mother said, "You naughty child.
Let's calculate the fuss and bother,
You've wrecked our game, you've upset Father,
Embarrassed us – of all the nerve,

You're getting just what you deserve."
And Babs cried out this final plea,
"Oh children, children, learn from me!
To live in peace this side of heaven,
Learn to answer eight times seven!
And to avoid the pits of hell,
Master seven eights as well!"
The arrows flew, she tried to dart,
But whirled about and clutched her heart,
Falling like a ton of bricks,
Wretched – sobbing, *"Fifty-six."*
So take a lesson from this child,
Living reckless, feckless, wild,
Ignorant, inept, unable,
Knowing not her eight times table.
She didn't know it needed knowing.
Now her ignorance is showing,
And in the wind her entrails blowing,
And her fluids overflowing.

Or take the case of Mitchell Glover,
(Names are changed to protect my brother)
In his hands would always be
A Nintendo, Gameboy, or Wii.
On the bus, lunchtime, recess,
He'd never glance from his DS.
He'd even play with it in class,

Foredooming his demise – alas!
One day during Geography,
(A class in which he got a "D" –
Not that Mitchell gave a hoot,
As far as grades the point was moot.
To him what mattered was his score,
Which was a million fifty four).
He sadly failed to pay attention,
Hearing not his teacher mention
Words we use for mud that flows
Down the sides of volcanoes,
And other words besides that save
A boy from stumbling to his grave.
When Teacher, then, proclaimed a treat –
A field trip, with picnic to eat –
The children cheered, got on the bus,
And soon were at Vesuvius.
Oh what fun the students had!
For every lass and every lad,
Was playing on infirma terra,
On the rim of the caldera.
Tossing 'round with squeals and calls,
Accretionary lava balls,
Prancing just like little foals,
Over venting fumaroles,
Collecting basalt, pumice stones,
Sliding down the cinder cones,

Hide-and-seeking with their mates,
On the vast tectonic plates
In the process of colliding –
All the better, then, for hiding!
All but one, that doltish boy,
Playing with his handheld toy,
Lounging up against the bus,
Ignoring all things igneous.
When suddenly there was a *boom!*
And ash and smoke rose in a plume,
And lava flowed down thick and red –
As from a wound, the magma bled.
And Teacher bellowed, "Have no fear!
There's not a whiff of danger here.
If you've listened well in school,
And paid attention, as a rule,
You'll not be bothered by this ooze.
Now let us don our running shoes."
She guided them with words volcanic.
There was no terror, fuss, or panic.
They understood her when she'd urge,
"Watch the pyroclastic surge!"
Tephra, kipuka, extrusion,
Nothing caused the least confusion.
But Mitchell Glover sat unheeding,
With the lava t'ward him speeding.
When Teacher yelled sounds most bizarre,

"Lahar! Lahar! Lahar! Lahar!"
And in reply, that little devil
Said, "I gotta pass this level!"
He didn't know what "lahar" meant –
Ejecta, lava bomb, or vent –
Though Teacher spoke plain as you please,
Mitchell just kept tapping keys.
So don't say Teacher was to blame
For Mitchell being set aflame,
And swept up in a lava slide,
And breathing hydrogen sulphide.
It wasn't her fault Mitchell went
Over an eruptive vent,
And that he shot into the air,
And didn't take sufficient care
To miss an airplane, and evade
A helicopter's whirring blade.
And Mitchell suddenly remembered,
(Just before he got dismembered),
In games an extra life is free,
But not so in reality.
And so his classmates ran, complaining,
For upon them Mitch was raining.
Back at the school the teacher had
To break the news to Mom and Dad.
And so she phoned them up, annoyed,
And said, "Our picnic's been destroyed!

When Mitch was blown to smithereens,
And scattered by volcanic means –
A finger here, intestines there,
Some nipples flying through the air,
Eyeballs, toenails, skin, and fat,
A spleen, a kidney, splat, splat, splat –
Well, so upsetting were the sights,
The children lost their appetites!"
"That's awful!" Mitchell's mom boohooed,
"All that waste of lovely food!"
"And furthermore," the teacher railed,
"Not only is Mitch dead – he's failed!"
"Quite right too," his mom said, "Since
He wouldn't study – now he's mince."
And as she blew her pretty nose,
She asked, "His last words – what were those?"
"Ah yes," said Teacher, "Mitch was screaming,
Just before his final creaming,
'The world must know before I fall
My high score was . . .' and that was all."
So take a lesson from this child,
Living reckless, feckless, wild,
Ignorant, inept, in flames,
Knowing not volcanic names.
He never learned he needed learning,
Nor did he quash his Gameboy yearning.
Now in his urn young Mitch is turning,

With his shame forever burning.

Or take the case of Lizzy Platt,
(Names are changed to protect my cat),
In school she got all As and Bs,
And rarely Fs, and never Gs.
And once she got an A plus plus
Plus plus plus plus – the genius!
And then from universities,
Liz got a load of PhDs,
And other letters that impart
The notion that you're really smart.
But though at school one basks in glory,
Degrees and marks are half the story.
The other half is common sense,
Without which one has no defence
Against the world, so base, so cruel,
So ready to dispatch the fool.
Poor Lizzy Platt was one of these,
No matter all her posh degrees,
For though in school she had great skill,
In life she was an imbecile.
Exhibit A: see little Liz
Race to school to write a quiz.
Her only thoughts are "Don't be late,"
And "lahar," and "seven times eight."
With spiral eyes, her gaze hypnotic,

All her moves like one robotic,
T'ward her fate she madly rushes,
Clutching books like secret crushes,
Akin to one snared in romance,
She's like a zombie, in a trance.
She cannot see the path beyond,
The fence, the bush, the tree – the pond,
She cannot see what's plain as day,
So focussed is she on her A.
So like a steeplechasing horse,
Traversing an obstacle course,
She leaps o'er flower, leaf, and frond,
And bashes tree, and slogs through pond,
Collecting burrs and prickly pear,
And pickets, streaming through her hair,
And in her pockets, fish and toad;
Thus comes Lizzy to a road.
Now – does she stop and look both ways?
Or does she wander in a daze
Onto the road, where cars are zooming,
And pain is sure, and death is looming?
Oh Lizzy! Will she stop and think
Before she ventures past the brink?
For though a scholar is what Liz is,
Even corpses can't write quizzes.
You'll be surprised to hear, no doubt,
That Lizzy did *not* blunder out.

She stopped, she listened, then her gaze
Proceeded to be cast both ways.
And there'd be nothing more to write
If only she'd looked left and right.
But with a brash, impatient frown,
Poor Liz looked up! And then looked down!
Imagine, then, the squeal of tires,
Screeching, squelching all desires,
Crushing Liz's good intentions,
Squashing her in two dimensions.
Imagine what an awful chore
To shovel up the guts and gore,
While passers-by through Liz must trudge,
Sliding, slipping on the spludge.
But no! If you'd imagined this
You'd be quite wrong, your thoughts remiss.
Because the street on which Liz strode
Was a runway, not a road.
And planes across the sky were spread
Like vultures, circling overhead.
Thus looking up made perfect sense,
And so Liz did, and ventured thence.
And no harm came to little Liz.
She got to school, she wrote her quiz,
She got her A, she got a pat
Upon her head, and that was that.
And life was jolly, life was swell,

Nothing happened, all was well –
Until that night when, sad to say,
Intoxicated by her A,
And deaf to all her mother's pleas,
Liz wouldn't eat her beans and peas.
All her veggies went uneaten!
And though cajoled and roundly beaten,
And though seen by the best physician,
Liz died next day of malnutrition.
So take a lesson from this child,
Living reckless, feckless, wild,
Ignorant, inept, infirm,
Food for buzzard, beetle, worm.
She didn't glean what needed gleaning,
Though bookish, studious, well-meaning;
Now scavengers are greedy, preening,
And on her corpse are trampolining.

Young person! Heed this dire warning
From three wretches whom we're mourning.
Do *not* be like these students who
Knew not what they did need to knew.
And there's the rub, you never know
What you might need to know, and so,
To stop your odds of death from growing,
Take my advice – become all-knowing.
And when you're sure of every fact,

And all your learning is exact,
And every datum's in your brain,
Go back and check it all again.
Then celebrate omniscience!
And also omni-commonsense!
And don't fret if you hear a boom,
And then see fireworks in the room.
Your brain is simply overloading,
And your little head's exploding.
One way or t'other your work is done!
God bless the eggheads, every one!

Study Guide

1. You may find it odd that Babs McLilty's parents took their little girl to a savage land on holiday. However, you yourself have undoubtedly been taken to just such places by your own parents without your realizing it. For example, Mexico is a popular holiday destination even though the Aztecs who lived there used to sacrifice their fellow citizens in the hopes that ripping their hearts right out of their bodies, without anaesthetic, would make life happier and more pleasant. That was a long time ago, you might argue, and you would of course be right – but "time" is something that we can't see, hear, smell, taste, or touch, and it is always uncomfortable to be separated from violent people ripping each other's hearts out by something that is completely invisible. In fact, since "time" is not in and of itself a "thing," you are separated from these savages by no thing. No thing at all. And many philosophers believe that time is unreal, an illusion, a mere concept – and it is always difficult to try and eat your *cabeza*-filled burrito, and to purchase your novelty sombrero and matching poncho, when the only thing that separates you from a marauding horde of crazy Aztecs is a concept.

   (By the way, you should know that *cabeza* means "head" in Spanish, thus a *cabeza*-filled burrito is a burrito stuffed with someone's head. The Mexicans have learned that an entire head wrapped in a burrito is extremely difficult to eat without special mouth-widening surgery, and that eating a head that hasn't been cooked is also a challenge for which most diners just haven't the patience. Therefore the head is roasted first, and it is either shrunk with a special machine called the *Cabeza-Shrinker 5000* – this almost never happens – or bits of it are sliced off and wrapped in the burrito with a little tomato and some iceberg lettuce – which oddly enough also comes in *cabezas*. All of this happens without the consent of the creature who donated its head, by the way, and who is now headless and therefore keeps walking into trees and can't remember where it parked. Thus, whether or not there are ancient Aztecs in the lobby of your hotel waiting to swing you over their llamas and take you to their temple for makeshift heart surgery, you may still find it hard to enjoy your burrito.)

The point is that Mexico is arguably a savage place, as is Hawaii, which is another popular tourist spot. The peoples of that region used to sacrifice each other as well, but worse still is that on the island of Hawaii itself, the Kilauea volcano has been continuously erupting since the year 1983. This may not be savage but is it safe? Oh, and if you think this is a minor eruption, think again – it's already caused earthquakes, annihilated towns, frightened a kitten, and destroyed the visitor centre and gift shop. It's hard to imagine parents taking their children on holiday to a place with an active volcano and no gift shop but it happens every day and no one thinks to question their motives or their sanity. *You* might question *your* parents' motives and sanity, however, if they decide to take you to Hawaii, and especially if they start talking about visiting the house of their friend Pele while they're there. This is because Pele is the goddess of volcanoes, and she actually lives in the steaming bowels of the volcano Kilauea itself, presumably without anything like a fridge or a snowcone machine. Living in steaming bowels without cooling appliances makes Pele so hot and unhappy that she might very well demand a blood sacrifice, and who could blame her. Thus Pele is a supernatural being best avoided, and if she invites you into her house, simply explain about your lava allergy and how, if you come into contact with it, you break out in charred flesh.

What is the most savage place that you have visited? Is it:

a.   your Uncle Morty's outhouse.

b.   the school cafeteria.

c.   the dank, gorilla-infested lowlands of east Borneo.

d.   the planet Nosegay.

2.   Many people believe that the answer to the question 7 times 8 is some number, largely unknowable, roughly between 36 and 81, and they are content not knowing

anymore about it than that. These are sensitive, non-nosey people who don't like to pry into the private lives of numbers, and think that if 7 and 8 have decided to multiply, it's none of their business what the outcome is. Other people gossip about numbers incessantly and are such snoops that they've seen, and even memorized, the times table right up to the twelves. They know about *pi*, and Graham's number, and the Fibonacci series, and the number of the beast, and even about *i*, which is that most useful of creatures – the imaginary number. *I* causes all kinds of problems, especially between math teachers and language arts teachers who often get into fruitless shouting matches like this one:

Math teacher: *I* is imaginary.
LA teacher: I *am* imaginary.
Math teacher: No – *i* is right.
LA teacher: No, you are wrong! You are not imaginary!
Math teacher: True, *u* is not imaginary. But *i* is.
LA teacher: *(howls, begins transforming into werewolf)*.
Math teacher: Listen. *I* is a number. Really *i* is.
LA teacher: *You* are crazy.
Math teacher: *I* is not crazy!

And so on. Such shouting matches usually end when the school bell rings (like at a boxing match), or when the janitor sprinkles their shoes with vomit powder and sweeps them away, or when one of them goes on maternity leave.

3. In the preceding poem, Babs' parents were said to be playing Cheat, a card game which, controversially perhaps, rewards players who are accomplished flimflammers and bamboozlers. The worst, most corrupt, stony-eyed players always win the game, and this is why police officers usually play a game of Cheat with suspected criminals in their interrogation rooms before a trial. It gives them valuable information about the suspect and, as a bonus, it's also lots of fun for everybody – and it is always a heartwarming, world-peace-inspiring sight to see police officers and their archenemies (dangerous criminals) having a laugh together. There's nothing like a game to bring diverse peoples with different interests together, is there, and it isn't usually long before the police officers are handing over their donuts and coffee, and the dangerous criminals are handing over their switchblades and stolen gems, their bombs and catapults and hostages. It's just too bad that if the criminals win the game they are handcuffed and taken to jail, and if the police win there is a lot of shuffling and whistling.

4. Many people are addicted to handheld games and play them when they ought to be paying attention to what's

going on around them. To determine if you yourself are addicted, answer this question: have you ever played a handheld game during one of the following events?

a. Your own birth.

b. An alien invasion, at which time the rest of your family was kidnapped and replicated so that now you are living with their zombielike clones. (Bonus question: does this perhaps explain anything?)

c. Hang gliding through sulfuric acid clouds during a lightning storm from the peak of Maxwell Montes to the plains of Ishtar Terra on the planet Venus.

If you answered *yes* to any of the above questions, it is safe to say that you are addicted to handheld games. If you answered *yes* to *all* of them, then you are to be congratulated on personally achieving spaceflight, but you might want to report the zombie-clone problem to the authorities and explain to your mother exactly how you got access to a handheld game while you were still a fetus.

5. Are you surprised to "learn" that a person can die of vegetable deprivation after only one missed serving? What exactly is your personal relationship with vegetables?

a. I love vegetables.
b. I hate vegetables.
c. We're not seeing each other right now.

6. The author of this poem evidently believes that to be on the safe side you should be omniscient – that is, you should know absolutely everything there is to know everywhere in the whole universe. The question is, do you yourself have godlike superpowers? If not, do you believe omniscience is a realistic goal for you personally?

Algebra

Dear Math Teacher:

I have a trifling, wee request that I would like to make,
A little thing that you could change so easily for my sake.
I'd do much better in your class,
    I'd flourish, bloom, and thrive,
If $n + 1$ was always 2 and x was always 5.

A weakness in your teaching
    is you can't make up your mind,
So I never know what number n or x have been assigned.
You keep it like a secret, under wraps and not for show,
But I'm a mathematician, not a mind reader you know.

Knowledge is the basis of a proper education,
How sad that math should be reduced
    to blind prognostication,
For I never know if x is five, five hundred, or five million,
That's why my answer's anywhere from one to a Brazilian.

You claim the answer lies within and I'm just unaware,
But I've looked in my head and still the answer isn't there.
And so it shall forever be, in vain I'll have to strive,
Till $n + 1$ is always 2 and x is always 5.

Lederhosen

Lederhosen is an amusing word which means "leather trousers" in German. Lederhosen are short pants that stop at the knee and are often held up by suspenders, because nobody, except maybe you and your sick friends, wants to see trousers falling down in little puddles all over the place. Lederhosen are often colourfully embroidered with leaves, flowers, and woodland animals (which perhaps explains why they are not popular in the toughest bars and on the school fields of North America). They also have a front flap that drops open – hopefully not of its own accord, and especially not when you are accepting the job of Prime Minister, shaking hands with the Pope, or saying your wedding vows. It is usually males who wear lederhosen, which is a pity as they are a snappy and attractive garment and ought to be worn by everyone, from humble cowherds to celebrity starlets.

It seems shortsighted to have only leather pants when there are so many other possibilities. Hence the following doggerel:

Next time you visit Germany,
    Please wear your finest lederhosen,
And if the language sounds funny,
    Then wear your best translatorhosen,
And if you are a little boy,

You might wear your first-graderhosen,
But if great age you do enjoy,
    You'll opt for grizzled grey-hairedhosen.
Who *are* you? Indiana Jones?
    Then wear your rugged raiderhosen.
Or are you one who nags and moans?
    Then wear annoyed Ralph-Naderhosen.
If you're a Judas, or a spy,
    You'll wear your shameful traitorhosen,
But if you're God of earth and sky,
    We'll worship your creatorhosen.

Lederhosen, latterhosen,
Leaderhosen, latherhosen,
Letterhosen, laterhosen,
Even alligatorhosen!

If plundering is your intent,
    Be sure to wear invaderhosen.
You'd best look twisted, tough and bent,
    I would suggest Darth-Vaderhosen.
    (And don't forget lightsaberhosen,
    A kind of neon laserhosen.)
To rule with force and stop dissent,
    Put on your fierce dictatorhosen.
But if you are from heaven sent,
    Wear medieval crusaderhosen.

And watch out for avenging knights,
  In righteous vindicatorhosen,
And to prevent some bloody fights,
  Escape in your evaderhosen.

Liederhosen, leiderhosen,
Liverhosen, lionhosen,
Lonerhosen, loserhosen,
Even Lego-userhosen!

Will you visit in September?
  I hope you've autumn lederchosen,
But if you visit in December,
  You're bound to get your lederfrozen.
And fun is fine, but what of work?
  You will need your labourhosen,
You can't decide to work or shirk?
  Put on your best debatorhosen.
Then if you think a job's for you,
  Perhaps put on your waiterhosen,
And if you like your collar blue,
  You might enjoy bricklayerhosen.
If making money is your aim,
  Put on your stock exchangerhosen,
But if philosophy's your game,
  Hold fast to Ockham's razorhosen.

So many hosen to write prose in!
Happy hose to banish woes in!
Cozy hose to put your toes in!
Heavy hose for when the snow's in!
Lemurhose a lemur goes in!
Lunarhose a U.F.O.'s in!
Lazyhosen to repose in!
Leperhose to decompose in!

So – when you visit Germany,
    Please wear your finest lederhosen,
Suspenders, flaps, embroidery,
    Lederhose are clothes to pose in.
And when you have to go back home,
    You'll be downhearted I'm supposin',
But ever in these trousers roam –
    The greatest beaus are those in hosen!

Bonus Hosen

1. You may be unfamiliar with both the liederhosen and the leiderhosen mentioned in the preceding poem. These are common so-called "misspellings" of lederhosen, and there are those among us (teachers, parents, orangutans) who think that they ought not to be used. Nonsense! Liederhosen means Song Pants – and should we not all possess a pair of pants that sing to us? How beautiful to awaken in the morning to one's pants perched on a chair and singing like Pavarotti! Or perhaps Song Pants are ones that we put on when we feel like bursting into song ourselves – a marvellous idea that surely raises liederhosen out of the category of a mistake. Human beings sing, after all, thus those who think that Song Pants are a mere "misspelling" are fundamentally antihuman, and should not be allowed to wear pants at all.

    Leiderhosen, however, means something like Sadly Pants and would probably be worn when we are feeling sorry, and brooding, and throwing ourselves onto our beds and sighing great sighs. It is then that we need our Song Pants most.

2. "And if you like your collar blue" is a reference to people we call blue-collar workers – that is, those people who do noble and heavy work with their hands such as brick-

laying, mining, and construction. White-collar workers work in offices and use their hands for only light work, such as typing and lifting coffee mugs to their lips. Other workers include pink-collar workers (teachers, nurses, flamingo-keepers), green-collar workers (environmentalists, farmers, leprechauns), gold-collar workers (lawyers, engineers, hosen poets), and puce-collar workers (flea circus employees). Although we know the colour of their collars, the colour of their lederhosen is anybody's guess.

3. You may not have fully understood the following line, "Or are you one who nags and moans? / Then wear annoyed Ralph-Naderhosen." Ralph Nader is a very important man who is, among other things, a "consumer advocate" – that is, a person whose job it is to test things in order to make sure they are safe, and if they're not, to wail like a police siren until something's done about it. For example, there was a time when some car manufacturers were making very unsafe cars (without steering wheels and brakes, I imagine) and it was Ralph Nader who made a colossal fuss about it, thus saving the lives of millions of careless motorists who might otherwise have crashed into trees or raced headlong over cliffs. Ralph Nader wants to protect us from everything that has the potential to harm us, from nuclear power plants to faulty lederhosen. He has made a successful

career out of full-time whining, a fact of which you should remind your parents the next time you are accused of doing the same.

4. Some of you may be surprised to learn that Ockham's razor is not, in fact, a sharp, bladed implement used by Mr. William O. Ockham to remove his whiskers. Ockham's razor is actually an idea, and it means that the simplest explanation is often the correct one. For example, let's say that upon looking into the bathroom cabinet, you are suddenly overcome by an urge to spray your father's shaving cream all over the place (or your mother's shaving cream – it would be presumptuous of me to assume that your mother is not a bearded circus lady.) Let's suppose that you go on a rampage and spray the wondrous lather inside your sister's backpack and the family minivan, all over the toaster and the family pet, and on your own head so that for a few glorious moments you look like a soft vanilla ice cream cone. Now, when your parents see you standing there looking like a Dairy Kween confection, they will naturally want an explanation – and when you tell them that you were overcome by an uncontrollable urge to spray shaving cream all over the place, they will understand and believe you. It is a simple explanation that takes all the facts into account – besides which it is a common enough compulsion, probably acted out by thousands of people

every day in this country alone. If instead, however, you tell your parents that the Shaving Cream Fairy came in the dark of night to shower you and your home with her blessings, then you have failed to apply Ockham's Razor and will likely lose your allowance, and your bathroom-cabinet privileges, because of it. (You may lose these anyway, of course, but at least you will not have lost your dignity – what's left of it, that is, as the shaving cream oozes over your forehead and into your eyes, enveloping you in a suffocating fluff that causes you to run around in circles, flapping your arms and foaming at the mouth like a rabid cloud.) What you have done by introducing a fairy into your explanation is to needlessly multiply assumptions, and instead of simply believing that you have urges identical to everyone else, your parents will be forced to assume that 1) fairies exist 2) they come to our homes and shower us with their blessings and 3) you are a nutbar and belong on a funny farm. So, Young Person, remember to apply Ockham's Razor in your thinking – no need to tell your teacher that a fire-breathing dragon ate your homework, for example, when it was really just the dog.

5. Are you, too, a student of hosen? Ladlehosen, firehosen, lavahosen, tazerhosen, lawyerhosen, leopardhosen, lobsterhosen, loiterhosen . . . hosenpfeffer? If you are a devoted fan of hosen, see if you can add to this list! (If

you are not a hosen-lover my heart bleeds for you, and I only hope you can dredge up some meaning and purpose in your sad life in the absence of lederhosen. Have you perchance considered dirndls?)

See you laterhosen!

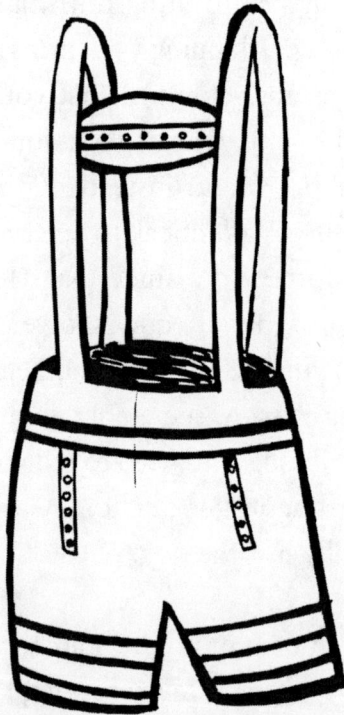

Mister Miserly

There was a Mister Miserly who wanted to be known
As lavish, though to churlish penny-pinching he was prone,
And so he called the children 'round and this is what he said,
"I've got a sweet if you can guess the number in my head.
And just to prove I'm not even the teensiest bit frugal,
I'll give a hint – the number is between *one* and a *googol,*"
(A number used by scientists and top-notch spelling champs,
And by collectors who collect an awful lot of stamps).
"I'm *sure* you'll guess the number now,"
The mean old miser hissed,
And chortled like a miser does behind a withered fist.
But right away a tiny tot whose name was Maximillian
Said, "I'll bet you're thinking of a duovigintillion."
"A duovigintillion!" Mister Miserly repeated,
And threw the sweet at little Max,
And walked away defeated.

Study Guide

Like the novemquinquagintillion, the quinquadragintilliard, and the phone number of the Mouse Dropping Medical Clinic And Pizzaria, the duovigintillion is sadly neglected. The duovigintillion, also known as 10^{69} to mathematicians, but simply as "Duey" to his friends, is a very, very large number, who, because of his size, has thighs that chafe when he walks, and has to buy two adjoining seats on airplanes. His doctor has tried to encourage him to get down to 10^{68} or even 10^{67}, but so far no luck.

Question: what are the odds that you'll be able to figure out the odds of little Maximillian guessing the exact number Mister Miserly was thinking of?

Mrs. Misery

There was a Mrs. Misery whose life was full of grief,
Because her little Reginald seemed dim beyond belief.
So to a posh psychiatrist she took him for a test,
The Doctor said, "I'm sorry,
But it's worse than you had guessed.
Not only is your Reginald a peabrain but I've found,
His deficits of temperament and character abound.
He's uncreative, visionless, complacent, feeble, weak,
He's in every thesaurus as a synonym for 'meek.'
He's passionless and unassertive, unproductive too,
He lacks direction, education, what we call 'IQ.'
He's reticent, standoffish, quiet, all he does is gawk,
I've never seen such secrecy, you can't get him to talk.
He's got no sense of teamwork and he isn't enterprising,
The fact he's got no self-esteem is not the least surprising.
He seems to have no sense of time and so he's always late,
He cannot manage people, organize, or delegate.
Your Reginald's a failure, Ma'am,
Though not evil or sinister,
But I'd bet my own mother
That he'll never be Prime Minister!"
Poor Mrs. Mis'ry wept
And gave the doctor quite a tidy sum,
Then took Reg in his bowl,
And brought him home to his aquarium.

Study Guide

Do you believe that the doctor in this poem was a quack, or perhaps even an actual duck and, if he was a waterfowl, do you think he showed considerable restraint in not eating Reginald?

First Contact

Young Person, you know that a good education
Prepares you for Life or (at least) graduation.
For high schools and low schools I've nothing but praise,
But still – there are things they don't teach there now'days.
For instance, Young Person, you've likely suspected
That alien life has not yet been detected.
And humans have only just been to the moon –
Or so your sly teachers would have you assume.
They don't want to tell you we've recently come
From Vega and Epsilon Geminorum.
And alien life? Why, we've already met!
But these are the facts they don't want you to get.
I guess they're afraid that if you knew the truth,
You'd embarrass us all in the manner of youth.
You'd joyride in spaceships while sniffing a glue stick,
And play foreign life forms your noisy rock music.
But I'm here to tell you what really took place,
When first we encountered new creatures in space.
It's time that you knew of this meeting profound,
And if any teachers start sniffing around
And asking you questions, pretend to be deaf,
Or fall to the carpet and fake your own death.
You know how they are, if you try to be clever,
They'll give you detention from now till forever.
And *I* don't want tutors and teachers galore

Stampeding like mastodons straight to *my* door.
Trust me – with something of this magnitude –
Keep it hush-hush, so you won't be pooh-poohed.

Here are the facts – it began with a probe,
Sent from the Earth to a far distant globe.
And on this world alien life was detected,
And scientists said, "This life must be inspected."
But who should be sent to salute these new creatures,
With possible eyestalks and other strange features?
Not scientists, surely! At least, not at first –
We didn't want aliens thinking the worst.
What if they thought we're *all* fashion defectors,
With goggles and lab coats and pocket protectors?
And what if they thought geeky hair is a trait?
And that we can't dance and we can't get a date?
What if they thought we all look like a dunce,
And speak with hand puppets, equations, and grunts?
No, we decided, the people to send
Would not call a lab rat or mouse their best friend.
We needed a person who'd shaken the hand
Of many a stranger, in many a land.
A person who'd shake even alien things –
Tentacles, eyestalks, antennae on springs –
Without getting into a terrible tizzy,
So we asked, if the Queen wasn't terribly busy,
Would she travel by rocket through wormholes in space,

In order to hail this new alien race,
And put up with possible light years of jet lag?
"Spiffing!" the Queen said, whilst grabbing her hand bag.*
We had our ambassador, now what we'd need
Was someone who flies with an excess of speed.
We hired a Captain from Russia somewhere,
A comrade named Ace with big pecs and slick hair,
And he looked at the Queen like a cheesecake buffet,
And he said, "Hey there, Babe, are you goink my vay?"
Elizabeth squealed like a girl of sixteen,
But just then another man burst on the scene.
America's president whooped a great, "Whoa!"
And Ace growled, "*Svedka!*" the Queen said, "What ho!"
The president said, "I'll be goin' with you.
If Russians are goin', then we're goin' too."
He climbed in the spaceship, his blood all aboil,
And said, "These here aliens better have oil,
'Cause Uncle Sam wants to do business with them."
Ace hissed, "*Stolichnaya!*" the Queen said, "Ahem."
But though there were tensions, these were the best

---

*For those of you who live outside the commonwealth
realm, you should know that the Queen's full name is
Elizabeth Alexandra Mary Windsor, and that she is the
much loved monarch of my country – Canada – as well as
some other countries, such as Papua New Guinea and
England.

Envoys to send on an alien quest.
Since each of the crew had anomalous features,
Who better for meeting weird alien creatures?
So that was our crew, an absurd potpourri –
The Captain, the President, Elizabeth, and me.

We set off at dawn in a vast fireball,
And travelled ten parsecs in no time at all.
And soon we arrived on the miniature planet –
Ace got out the Gizmo 3000 to scan it.
And sure enough alien life was revealed,
Apparently standing about in a field.
"That's tickety boo!" said the Queen, "Let us send
Some crumpets and tea to our alien friend,
And put in a note that says, 'How do you do?
So sorry for this billy-ho ballyhoo,
But the Queen is receiving aboard her spaceship,'
Then end, 'Cheerio, toodle-oo, and pip-pip.'"
Ace lovingly wrote down each word from the Queen,
Then added, "Vee also give Russian cuisine.
Sauerkraut, chicken Kiev, maybe borsch,
And maybe vee gotta have wodka, of coursh."
With sceptre in hand Liz said yes to her chum,
By dubbing him knight and then whacking his bum.
But love was disrupted with, "Looky here now,
Them aliens want some *American* chow."
The president said, "What they want is a steak,

A bucket o' chicken, a hotdog, a shake,
Give 'em some grub they can eat in their car –
That's how America's gotten so far –
Just make sure it's loaded with sugar and fat,
And be sure to ask, 'D'ya want fries with that?'"
Out of the freezer he took steak and buns,
And said, "Hope they like these 'cause they're the last ones."
He said grace and filled up a Styrofoam bin,
Ace muttered, "*Gdańska,*" the Queen sipped some gin.
And off went the note with the foodstuffs attached,
And then we all waited with tension unmatched.
We waited and waited and waited some more,
The President slumped, then he started to snore,
I looked out the porthole, then started to pace,
Ace gazed at Lizzy, and Liz gazed at Ace.
I looked at my watch – it had stopped at 10:10 –
Thank goodness the Queen had brought with her Big Ben.
Its Westminster chimes rang out quarter to three,
So Ace drank some vodka, the Queen drank some tea,
The President woke with a great oikish snort,
And gobbled a sub, drinking Coke by the quart.
And three became four, and the President stewed,
And four became five, and Ace got in a mood,
And five became six, and the Queen became vexed,
You get the idea, you can guess what came next.
By seven they felt like they'd waited for years,
And they were fatigued, discomposed, bored to tears.

And anticipation became disappointment,
The President said, "There's a fly in the ointment.
These Yahoos won't give us a *nope* or a *yup*,"
And he pleaded, "Come on – can't we just blow 'em up?"
"Indeed!" said the Queen, "What a boorish rebuff!"
And we would have gone home, just flown off in a huff,
When I humbly suggested it might be the case
That they couldn't read English way out here in space.
"Humph," said Her Majesty, rife with dismay,
"English or not – one responds, *sil vous plait.*"
"Yup," said the President, grabbing a reed,
"A whuppin' is what these E.T.s seem to need."
"*Nyet, nyet,*" said the Captain, "Vith them vee discuss,
And find out vhy they not speak Eenglish to us."
And so we decided to open the case
And question these little green men face to face.
Their judges? The cream of our society –
The Captain, the President, Elizabeth, and me.

We stepped from the ship to a meadow of grass
And flowers, beside a small lake smooth as glass.
Ace looked at the scanner and cried, "Now they come!"
What we felt was excitement times ten, and then some.
For this was the moment that we'd go *beyond,*
And jump to the ocean of Life from the pond.
As species go, humans were babies at best,
Sucking our thumb, spitting up on our chest,

From Earth's spinning cradle we'd crawled a long distance,
Right into the living room of our existence.
And now here we were, all grown up, so to speak,
You couldn't help pinching humanity's cheek,
And tickling its tum-tum, and giving it a twirl,
And cooing, "So who's a big boy and big girl?"
With *aliens* we were about to converse!
Children, at last, of the *whole* universe!
So finally over a hilltop one showed,
And Ace cried "*Blavod*!" the Queen said, "Well I'm blowed!"
However, the President climbed on a stand,
And read from the speech that he held in his hand.
"Fellow Americans, I simply can't wait
To welcome you all to this fifty-first state.
We welcome yer oil, we'll take it for free,
In exchange for which we'll give you democracy."
The President paused, then looked up from the page,
His jaw dropped, his heart sank, right there on the stage.
The President huffed, "Well just looky here now –
Doggone it that alien looks like a cow."
And then other life forms came o'er in a slow line,
And all of them ungulates – all of them bovine.
So that was the reason that they didn't call –
It turned out they couldn't speak English at all!
So it wasn't because they were stupid or lazy,
Or because English grammar and spelling are crazy.
They couldn't speak French, or Pig Latin, or Scottish,

Which since they were cows wasn't really so oddish.
"Vait, vait!" said the Captain, "They're *looking* like cows,
The vay that they moo and they chew and they browse,
But looking and being is nyot the same thing –"
Thank goodness that Ace had remembered to bring
The Doodad 5000, with communicator,
Mind-reading option, and instant translator.
He plugged in a plug and he switched on a switch,
He cranked up a crank and he hitched up a hitch,
He dialled a dial from *human* to *other*,
He pushed flashing buttons one after another,
And turning a knob to the mind reading setting,
Said, "Now we are communicating, I'm betting."
Advancing, the President made a slight bow,
And slowly, with voice raised, said "How now brown cow?
Speaky you oil? It comes in a tanker?"
And Ace sighed, *"Popov!"* the Queen said, "What a *wanker*."
And then the Queen spoke and said, "How do you do?"
And shockingly, none of the creatures said "Moo."
We heard them inside our own heads, clearly speaking –
So this was the moment for which we'd been seeking!
What would they say to this gracious invasion,
On this benign and historic occasion?
While still staring dumbly and swishing her tail,
The bellwether creature stepped off of the trail.
She looked, as beasts do, dignified and demure,
Her first words to us were, "Delighted, I'm sure.

Forgive us for standing about in the mud,
But we're all rather busy now, chewing the cud."
The President whooped and yelled, "My lucky day!"
And pushing Her Majesty out of the way,
And elbowing Ace so he fell in the soil,
Said, "Let's do business now – bring out yer oil!"
The creature contentedly chewed on some grass,
And answered his question by passing some gas,
And saying, "I'm sorry, we've none of that here,
We have only water that flows crystal clear.
We drink it," she added, her words falling flat.
The President said, "Well, all right – we'll take that."
"Now, now, where's our manners?" the Queen interjected,
Feeling these creatures should not be subjected
To bilious, imperialist, American greed,
So she said, "To *Great Britain*, of course, you'll accede –
You'll love Monty Python, the gardens at Kew,
And Stonhenge and pubs, Mr. Bean, Dr. Who –"
The President bellowed, and he tried to slug her,
Ace threatened, "*Khmelnaya!*" the Queen said, "Oh,bugger."
The aliens, meanwhile, peacefully lowing,
Said, "It's been swell, but perhaps we'll be going."
"Vait!" cried the Captain, "You stay for a drink,
And tell us – our presents – so vhat did you think?"
"Well," said the ungulate, "thanks for the thought,
But we were confused by these things that you brought.
For instance – what's *this*?" and she strolled to the lake,

Where lay the President's bloody, raw steak.
The President said, "Why that there is some meat,
It's what we Americans most like to eat."
The Queen said, "In Britain we eat many tons,
And ground up it tastes simply grand between buns."
"Ya," added Ace, "Vee are eating the cow,"
At which point the alien furrowed her brow.
"And what is a cow?" she asked tentatively,
Ace pulled out a picture – the beast said, "Dear me.
You eat one another? Is that what you do?"
"No, no!" cried the Queen, "that is simply not true!
We only eat *nonhuman* creatures you see . . ."
"Creatures," she asked, "who look something like me?"
"Well," said the Queen, "it is true that you seem
Like you'd go with potatoes and fresh sour cream,
But looking and being is *nyot* the same thing –"
She nodded at Ace and he felt like a king –
"For instance, although you might think this is daft,
A cow has *four* stomachs – two fore and two aft.
It's silly – if you want to laugh go ahead –"
"We have four stomachs," the alien said.
"But true cows make milk in a thing called an udder –"
And Ace interjected, "For feed one anudder –"
"You see?" said the Queen, "You're not like that a bit,"
"Our milk," said the beast, "is the best you can get."
"But cows are unclean, they've got lice in their coat!
They can't talk or sing and they've not got the vote!

They can't use a tool! They can't drive a bus!"
"You're saying," the beast said, "that they're just like us."
"No, no," said the Queen, "a cow's IQ is slight –"
"As for us," said the beast, "we're not overly bright."
"Well that takes the biscuit!" she said with a huff,
The President said, "I think we've heard enough.
Just one final question, you may find it odd,
But we need to know – do you believe in God?"
"Who?" asked the beast, which was a mistake,
The President said, "Well that done take the cake.
These creatures have nothin' in which to believe in,
Not only is this here a cow – it's a heathen."
"I'm not knowing what you are talking about,"
Said Ace, "But of steak vee are now running out."
"You don't mean – " the Queen said, with gloved hand to lips,
But all she could think of was fresh steak and chips.
"They may not have oil," the President said,
But this third world planet has somethin' instead.
Oh they've got resources, a goodly supply,
And right now I'm lookin' one straight in the eye."
"I think we'll be going," the alien said,
And over the hill, one by one, they all fled.
But who ran behind them with ravenous glee?
The Captain, the President, Elizabeth, and me.

So that's why, Young Person, you'll not hear this story,
Some bleeding heart herbivores think it's too gory.

They say that we should not have gone to their residence,
Contacted them, and then eaten the evidence.
But alien DNA proves what they were –
Bovines – with flesh fit for a connoisseur.
And we know that Earth-cows think just like they do –
The Doodad 5000 works fine with them too.
So they really were cows, so it's really okay,
That we met them and ate them all on the same day.
It wasn't a meeting you'd say was . . . auspicious –
But the party was grand – and the food was delicious!

Note: Lest you think I shamelessly made them up, the Russian words used in this poem are all authentic, and are all proper brand names of Vodka.

Study Guide

1. Besides our first contact with aliens, what other important information do you think teachers are keeping from you? For example, have you heard of any of the following events?

   a. The infamous leprechaun uprising of 1753.

   b. The Great Invisible Spirit Hoohaw of 1986 – this took place in a barn that, for a hundred years, was haunted by goats.

   c. The Dinosaur Olympics, held every four years since the late Cretaceous.

   d. The recent discovery of Zeus, god of the sky and of thunder, living in a modest bungalow with about 50 of his children by his godly and heroic exploits, and having been dumped by his long-suffering wife, Hera, goddess of marriage (and significantly, of cows). Perhaps you saw the six o'clock news the day that Hera left Zeus in her wagon pulled by peacocks. If you did not see the news that day, do you think it was because your parents turned off the TV and distracted you with ice cream and computer games on the advice of your teachers? Do you think your teachers don't want you to know about Zeus because he condemned Prometheus to have his liver eaten every day by a giant eagle, and this might give you "ideas?" Do you think your teachers don't want you to know about Hera because they do not have sufficient scientific imagination to explain exactly *how* she was swallowed whole by her father at birth and subsequently vomited back up with her siblings? (Bonus question: do you think Hera was wrong to leave Zeus, even though he once dangled her upside down from the sky and everyone could see her knickers?)

2. Do you think that the Queen of England shouldn't use naughty words, even if they do make excellent rhymes? What are *your* favourite bad words? If you own a parrot, have you ever tried to teach it to say your favourite bad words? If you succeeded, did your parents ground you or both you and your parrot? If they grounded your parrot, do you think this was fair? Do you reserve these bad words for special occasions, such as when you accidentally apply glue-gun glue to your own finger, or do they make up the majority of the words in your vocabulary? Where did you learn these bad words? Circle one:
   a. From the big kids at the back of the school bus.
   b. From my Dad.
   c. From my parrot.
   d. From poetry.

Spell these words and discuss loudly.

3. Do you think the author of this poem was lazy for not looking up real Russian words but using the names of alcoholic beverages instead? Now that you know the names of various brands of vodka, do you believe that you are on the slippery slope leading to the life of the down-and-out drunkard, and that because of this poem you will someday find yourself living in a cardboard box under a bridge with only a bottle of *Stolichnaya* to keep you warm at night? Have you been previously corrupted by the song "Ninety-nine Bottles of Beer on the Wall" anyway and so, really, it's already too late for you and we should all just save ourselves?

4. Do you think the Queen's royal consort, her husband Prince Philip, might be angry about the Queen's relationship with Ace? Would it make you nervous to be married to an English monarch who, in previous times, would simply cut your head off if you annoyed her, even a little bit? What if you weren't entirely sure if she still had that power or not? Like Prince Philip, would you act merry on the outside, just in case?

5. Who do you think the narrator thinks she is anyway, and why did *she* get to go on a voyage with some of the most powerful people on the planet? What do you think of the narrator on a personal level? Do you think she has some strange ideas about scientists, teachers, and American

presidents? After reading this poem, do you have an urge to send the narrator money?

6. Do you agree with the narrator that it really was okay to eat the alien cows? If you disagree, do you do so on the basis that it is always bad manners to eat others while you are representing Earth on a diplomatic mission? For example, would it be wrong of a Canadian diplomat to go on a state-sponsored visit to, say, Turkey, and then to eat all of the inhabitants of that great nation? What if they are all turkeys, as I assume they are? Does this make a difference? Discuss the idea of speciesism and the role it plays in our food choices.

    (Speciesism is the word we use to describe discrimination on the basis of species, and explains why many people will eat Bessie and Porky, but not Mittens or Rover.)

7. Do you eat animals? If so, do you find they struggle quite a bit when you try to get them on your fork? Have you found a way to overcome this difficulty?

8. Would you like to be eaten? Why or why not? Do you think nonhuman animals like to be eaten? Why or why not? Do you think rocks like to be eaten? Why or why not? Have you personally eaten a rock? Did you do so because you are a chicken and you need rocks for your

gizzard? Have you put a rock in any other orifice – for example, have you ever inserted a rock into your nose? Have you inserted a chicken?

9. If you answered *yes* to this last question, is the chicken still in your nose? Should we wait while you go and give your nose a big blow? Would you personally like to be inserted into someone's nose? Do you think that poor chicken liked it? I mean, honestly . . .

10. Did you know that many people don't eat animals at all because they are vegetarians, and that many others don't eat them because they are vegans and refuse to eat or to use *anything* that originates from an animal, such as leather, wool, silk, or beeswax? Most people who are vegans make this choice out of love and compassion for animals, but other people who are vegans are actually aliens from the star Vega and carry probes and powerful ray guns. Can you tell the difference between the two types of vegans? Discuss the implications of a possible mixup between vegans and vegans during a social engagement.

11. Do you think it is practical to bring a clock with a bell the size of Big Ben onto a spaceship? Given that the clock tower weighs approximately 8,667 tonnes, and a rocket carrying this weight would burn fuel at a rate of about 30

tonnes a second, do you think this is this a good use of the Earth's resources? If you said *no,* are you the teensiest bit afraid that Queen Elizabeth might cut your head off? Do you plan to act merry and bumble through the rest of your days regardless of this fact?

When Mummy Tucks Me In

When Mummy tucks me in at night
I feel like I'm in heaven,
With teddy, blanky, milky drink,
Too bad I'm 47.

When Daddy Gives Me Uppies

When Daddy gives me uppies
Then I soar just like a plane,

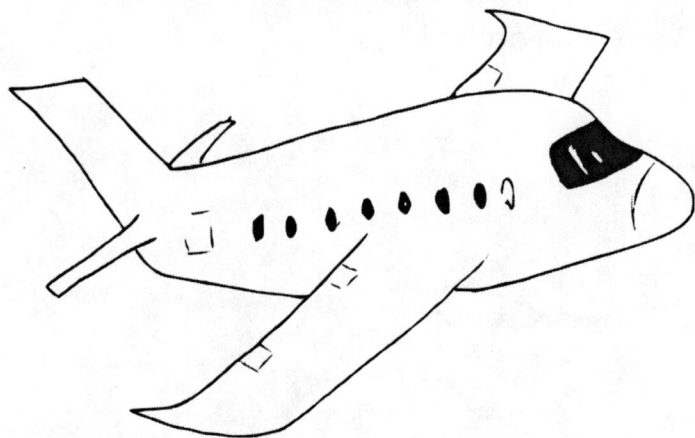

It's bad I weigh five hundred pounds,
But good he has a crane.

When Auntie Takes Me To The Zoo

When Auntie takes me to the zoo
I laugh, and run, and play
With lions, since she always locks me in
and runs away.

When Uncle Takes Me Into Space

When Uncle takes me into space
I get a rocket ride!
I only wish I had some air
and was allowed inside.

Chant

Note to teachers: this chant should be performed during a field trip, using sticks and bongo drums around a blazing fire in the dead of night during a new moon. There should be jungle noises – insects chirping, monkeys howling, jaguars panting. Fire ants should be a problem. Little faces should be streaked with war paint, and silly string should be placed carefully to look like ritual scarring. Girls should wear gold bangles and seashell necklaces with grass skirts and coconut shell bikini tops. Boys should wear lederhosen.

Remind the children that, as usual, there will be a quiz afterwards – in this case, a quiz with only one question, and the question should be phrased thus: all of these words have vowels, consonants, and capital letters – that much is obvious. But all of these words, except the last two, have something else in common. What is it? (And, by the way, don't be thrown off track by the fact that there is occasional repetition of a word – sometimes, though not always, for purely rhythmic effect.)

Amakihi Apapane Weka Kaka Akekee,
Chachalaca Tui Oo Oo Piha Kea Kiskadee.

Boubou Ou? Bokikokiko! Ou Ou Ou Ou Kokako,
Mossie Motmot Knot Knot Chat Chat Caracara Omao.

Doradito Mao Mao Inca Sora Takahe,
Colasisi Ifrit Nene Iiwi Pewee Suiriri.

Mango Vanga Wongo-wanga Mamo Drongo Maleo,
Potoo Potoo Hoopoe Hoopoe Hylacola Kakapo.

Hemispingus? Veery Ouzel! Huet-huet Nukupuu!
Shikra Besra Purple Roller Prion Tyrant Jabiru.

Treepie Limpkin Pitohui Ani Galah Ruff Ruff Ruff!
Shama Minla Aracari Dunlin Sungem That's Enough!

If you haven't figured out the riddle yet, here's a hint –
the previous words are all names of . . . something. Perhaps
a chant in Latin will make it clearer. (Note to all of you
native Latin speakers: pronounce as in English.)

Nothocercus bonapartei Napothera crispifrons,
Bubo bubo Pauxi pauxi Melanerpes flavifrons.

Melospiza melodia Alectura lathami,
Mitu mitu Apus apus Polyplectron germaini.

Francolinus streptophorus Troglodytes rufulus,
Otus scops Poospiza caesar Nothocercus julius.

Turdus boulboul Pica pica Loriculus flosculus,
Todus todus Jynx torquilla Hemicircus concretus.

Turnix hottentotta Perdix perdix Upupa epops,
Anser anser Myrtis fanny Hemitriccus zosterops.

Megalaima incognita Aburria aburri
Sphyrapicus thyroideus Larus livens – What are we?

?

Find the answer on the following page.

We are all names of

Species
of
Bird!

Study Guide

Many people are amazed to discover that there are not one hundred, or one thousand, but at least *ten thousand species* of bird on our planet alone. Given that many people can name only 25 species, tops – and often pad their lists with names such as Toucan Sam, Big Bird, and Tweety – this is an alarming fact, and suggests that some people don't know much about the planet they live on. Many people feel that there are just *too many* bird species, and they want the government minister in charge of Evolutionary Affairs to do something about it. These people are also in favour of an immediate reduction in the number of phases of the moon, arguing that because a new moon is invisible it's no good to anyone, and they don't want any more of their tax dollars wasted on it.

Smug people, who claim to know about everything *except* birds, can still often be stumped by the following list: Punchinello, Short Flash, Tricolour Pied Flat, Indian fritillary, Orange staff sergeant, Sullied sailor, and Chestnut Bob – all names of species of butterfly, as you may have guessed. Still other people who brag about their vast knowledge of birds and butterflies begin to sweat unattractively at these words: Little Dumbbell, Tarantula, Bubble, Lagoon, Keyhole, Pencil, Heart, Veil, Pacman, Trifid, Cat's Eye, Checkmark, Homunculus, Clownface, and (best of all) Dark Doodad. These, of course, are all names of nebulae, but many people who hear of *Antares and the Rho Ophiuchus dark cloud* believe that this is a rock band and not a magnificent celestial system.

Question: do you now feel inspired to fill in the gaps in your own knowledge? Do you intend to:

a. study black holes by travelling to a few of them (NB: bring a flashlight!).

b. learn the names of every one of the elements of the periodic table, and add more as you discover them in the cracks of your house and the folds of your skin?

c. discover the surname of every earthworm on your block?

The Story of Noah's Ark

There was a man named Noah who was pious as you please,
And meeker than a kitten, and holier than Swiss cheese,
As upright as a mountain, as lowly as a pebble,
So sheepish that he made a sheep look like a lawless rebel,
A veritable teacher's pet, and requisite soft touch,
The perfect choice for gath'ring beasts,
And building arks and such.
And so God said to Noah, "Son, this is your lucky day.
I'm going to drown all living things, except for you – hooray!
There're just three things you need to do,
You'd best begin this minute;
Collect two of each species,
Build an ark,
And put them in it."
And Noah started sweating,
And his thoughts convulsed and swirled,
And God said, "It won't be that bad, it's just one little world!"
"But God," said Noah, "you know me, I'm not a man to fuss,
It's just that I've got allergies to cats and bee stings, plus
I'm *six hundred years old*," he argued, as it started raining,
And God said, "I'm *eternal*, but you don't hear me complaining.
Just think of all the travel! The adventure and the fun!
Now get to work, my devotee, and call me when you're done."
So Noah, heavyhearted, built an ark of wood and glue,
Then started catching creatures for his massive floating zoo.

Oh, pity Noah! with the Earth to circumnavigate,
Dressed in a safari suit, his pockets stuffed with bait,
Travelling the world upon a horse like Don Quixote,
Setting sneaky Acme traps, like Wile E. Coyote,
Scampering through meadows, butterfly net in his hand,
Belly-flopping on his prey, in water, and on land,
Tempting rodents into traps with little bits of cheese,
Running scared from scorpions, and bulls, and killer bees,
Pussyfooting into caves, and scrabbling in the mud,
Looking under every stone, in every flower bud,
Searching every crevice, every pond and bit of sludge,
For animals of *every* stripe, and spot and swirl and smudge!

Bilbies, dik-diks, kakas, cranes and kinkajous and coots!
Aye-ayes, drongos, fossas, Turkens, porcupines and newts!
Wombats, dippers, Whiskered Flowerpeckers,
Snipes and stoats!
Smelts and smews and wolverines
And auks and yaks and shoats!

Noah searched the whole world o'er
For life in every form,
And at a time when transport trucks
And planes were not the norm!
To get a box of dingos, say,
He'd go by foot and skiff,
But that meant *months* of travel home,

At which point they'd be stiff!
And sometimes crates of brutes
Would rip each other limb from limb,
And then they'd look at Noah, bust the crate,
And go for him!
Or sometimes it was peckish Noah, like some wild boar,
Who'd polish off the creatures, and be forced to go get more.
Plus it wasn't easy telling animals apart,
At least two thousand kinds of kindred rodents for a start!
Forty thousand spiders!
Eighty thousand snails and slugs!
Sixty thousand vertebrates!
A million kinds of bugs!
As much as thirty million species over all the planet,
But Noah soldiered on, with heart of gold and will of granite.

Shoebills, spoonbills, thorny devils, kangaroos and gnus!
Eyelash vipers, Jesus lizards, kakapos and shrews!
Beavers, boobies, dinos, dodos, bandicoots and crakes!
Dumbo rats, chinchillas, woodchucks, unicorns and snakes!

And oh! the things that Noah had to know a lot about,
Like how to tell a grizzly from a black bear by its snout!
And how to tell the difference between eighty breeds of cat,
And how to tell a wombat by its cubic wombat scat.
Koala bears eat leaves, he learned, but never eat the bark,
And as for tapeworms, squeamish Noah had to *be* the ark!
Still even though he had to know as much as his creator,

As huge as all his learning was, the danger was yet greater!
He had to capture vampire bats in guano-slicked abodes!
He had to know that suicidal ants will just explode!
He had to capture cheetahs
And get leashes 'round their necks!
He had to flip o'er hippos to identify their sex!
And just when Noah thought he must be done
Then God would say,
"Not yet – you've missed an aphid,
On a leaf,
In Paraguay."

Pythons, pufflegs, fruitbats, meerkats,
Penguins, blue-tongued skinks!
Turkeys, turtles, Fairy armadillos, Manx and minks!
Crocs, okapis, cockatoos and Red-necked Phalaropes!
Pronghorns, pandas, gobies, yetis, Bongo antelopes!

How happy Noah must have been with every beast aboard,
Sailing o'er the flooded Earth, a rainbow as reward.
And of three hundred kinds of dove,
He threw one off the boat,
To look for land (amongst the billion corpses now afloat),
And when the dove did not return,
He knew he'd found the shore!
But when the shore turned out to be
A mountain, Noah swore!

Oh why did God deposit him at twenty thousand feet,
Without a carabiner, or a crampon, or a cleat?
A lesser man than Noah might have said, "Enough's enough!"
But we know men like Noah
Are composed of sterner stuff.
Instead he blew a trumpet,
And then wearing full regalia,
Personally ushered the marsupials to Australia!

At least – that's how the story goes,
And yet I've always wondered,
If, when God first spoke to Noah,
While the heavens thundered,
Saying, "Noah, do this task,
I swear you won't regret it!"
I wonder if he laughed,
And walked away,
And said, "Forget it."

Study Guide

1. Noah was 600 years old when God asked him to build a
   boat the size of a shopping mall, to travel the world
   collecting a male and female of as many as thirty million
   species, and then to keep them from eating each other,
   and him. Do you believe the fact that Noah was 600
   years old actually makes the story much funnier than it
   already is? Does it amuse you, as it does me, to picture a
   600-year-old man building penguin traps, balancing
   unsteadily as he tries to entice bored-looking Bighorn
   Sheep off their ledges, or perhaps standing forlornly on
   a dusty road holding a lizard tail while the lizard scarpers
   off? Are you glad that Noah was not, say, 35, because it
   is much funnier to think of a 600-year-old man pumping
   his scrawny little arms and legs as he runs away from a
   couple of Komodo Dragons, all the while trying to shake
   a Gila Monster off his hand after it's bitten him and
   won't let go? Explain why this is tragically hilarious, as
   well as the image of Noah peering through watery eyes,
   long-since clouded over by cataracts, in an attempt to
   determine the gender of two midges.

   Also, in light of Noah's advanced age, do you now
   believe that your own grandparents are shockingly lazy?
   In order to win back your respect, do you intend to give
   them ark blueprints and a zoo pass for Christmas, with
   instructions to "Get cracking?"

2. God chose Noah to do His bidding because he was the most holy and good man around. If you believe in God, and you yourself are holy and good, are you now thinking of doing something really awful just to ensure that God doesn't pick you for anything? Or, if you do hear God's voice, do you plan to hide under your desk or behind a tree?

3. Later on in Noah's life he was sleeping without any clothes on (pyjamas had not yet been invented) when his son Ham entered the room without knocking. Noah, who was about 800 years old at this time, and so probably looked like a big white raisin with eyeballs, was madder than a wet hen about this, and so he made Ham, and all of his descendants for the rest of eternity, be the slaves of his brothers.

    Question: which do you think is worse – having an 800-year-old raisin with eyeballs for a dad, being made your brothers' personal slave, or being given the name Ham? What if Noah's last name was "Burger?" Do you think he was trying to curse Ham with a joke name? Do you think a joke name is an effective punishment for someone who can't seem to learn to knock?

4. Do you think Noah's friends helped him collect animals for the ark, making the job go just ever so much quicker? If so, do you think Noah said to his friends, "Here's the

plan everyone – we're going to build an ark, fill it with animals, and then God's going to kill you." Do you think Noah mumbled the last few words? Or do you believe Noah sugarcoated the truth by letting his friends put all of their belongings onto the ark so that they themselves believed they would be going? If Noah did this, do you think he felt a little guilty afterwards using all their stuff?

5. In the original story of Noah and the ark, the billions upon billions of rotting and bloated human and animal carcasses floating in the sea are never mentioned. Do you believe that ignoring this grim fact was a marketing decision? Do you think it would have been just too expensive to include a large number of plastic animals, with an X over each eye, for each of the millions of Noah's Ark bath toys?

6. We now know that telling species apart can sometimes be fiendishly difficult, and it is often only possible through DNA testing – which was only invented in the 1980s, and so was about five thousand years too late to do Noah much good (unless, in addition to building wallaby traps, Noah also built a time machine and could therefore travel into the future – and why should he not, as it doesn't make the story any more incredible). Biologists are forever lumping creatures together when they find some that actually belong to the same species, or more

often, splitting species apart when it becomes evident that although two creatures may look alike, they don't belong to the same species at all. In addition to this inconvenient fact, there also exist long *chains* of a *single* species, but the species gradually morphs so that, when the two ends of the chain meet up, the creatures at the beginning and end of the chain no longer belong to the same species! This is called a ring species, and it gives taxonomists, who are the people whose business it is to classify animals, one big collective pain in the *Equus asinus*.

In light of this complexity, do you now believe that it is obvious that Noah *didn't* tell the animal species apart because, in actual fact, he didn't have to? Is this because God must have magnetized the animals that he wanted to survive, and so they were attracted to the ark by a powerful force? Do you now believe, as I do, that this force was so powerful that it made all of the animals fly through the air at top speed, sometimes hitting the ark with a thunk and a disappointing splat? Does it make you happy, as it does me, to imagine Noah, seeing yet another pair of bewildered animals speeding like missiles toward the ark, taking cover and yelling, "Elephants at six o'clock! Incoming! Incoming!"

7. Some people believe that Noah didn't collect the insects. If Noah didn't do this, how did they survive?

a.   On the backs of accommodating whales.
b.   In flying space arks.
c.   They were recreated after the flood by one of God's minions, who couldn't read a manual, got completely mixed up, and so put the skeletons on the outside.

8. Like Noah, do you yourself sometimes hear God speaking to you? If so, how do you know it's Him?
a.   Well . . . it *sounds* like Him . . .
b.   If He tells me to do good, I know it's Him. If He tells me to do bad, I know it's my neighbour with a voice changer.
c.   There's only ever me and the cat in the room, and I've ruled out the cat.

9. How do you believe God drained the Earth after the flood?
a.   He pulled the plug.
b.   He sucked the water up through a straw, flung it out into space, and that's how Saturn's rings were formed.
c.   He flushed it through a wormhole in space, much to the chagrin of the space worms.

Touching

Once upon a dinner time
(Of sweet potatoes – mashed, sublime,
Of gravy, peas, a little meat)
There was a boy who wouldn't eat.
His peas, you see, had run amuck,
And by the sheerest worst of luck,
Like reckless ships on waters wavy,
Ventured forth into the gravy.
Upon the seas of stormy brown,
Many peas did sink, and drown.
Still others found potato mountain,
Via gravy stream and fountain,
And at its buttered base they died,
In a mashed potato slide.
Those peas remaining tried to row,
Onto a slice-of-ham plateau,
But those who made it to the pork,
Were promptly squashed beneath a fork.
Unlucky peas! Disgraced and beaten!
Mashed to death and never eaten!
Tortured, oozing, gloppy, sticky!
And all because of Mister Picky.

Mister Picky (that's the boy
Placed on god's green earth to annoy)
Didn't ask for very much –

Only that his foods not touch.
They couldn't mingle, meet, converge,
No foodstuffs were allowed to merge.
He'd make a fence of celery,
Preventing foods from roaming free,
Or with his carrots make a line,
So that his foods could not combine.
But if a food dare conjugate,
With other foods upon the plate,
The boy would just refuse to eat it –
Wouldn't digest or excrete it.
Let's say a noodle touched a bean,
(An act revolting, foul, obscene)
He'd then not touch his fettuccini,
Since his fork was slightly beany.
Or if his custard touched his bun,
He'd quickly dial 9-1-1,
"Emergency!" he'd gasp, all flustered,
"My bun's impinging on my custard!"
Or if a grape brushed past a prune,
He'd have to kill it with his spoon.
To make sure it was dead he'd bomb it,
Then drown it in a flood of vomit.

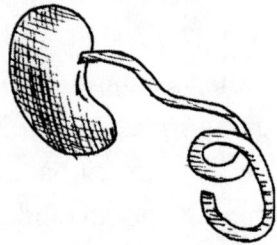

Worse than this would often follow,
When the imp refused to swallow,
And being his primary cooks,
His parents lived on tenterhooks.

For when the dinner bell would jingle,
If two foodstuffs dared commingle,
He'd grab his knife, point at the ooze,
Point at his Mum, and shout, *"J'accuse!"*
Through gritted teeth he'd say, "My yam
Is butting up against my ham.
Do you concede that you well knew
About this entrée rendezvous?
And what is *this?"* he'd hold the knife
Up against his father's wife,
"You thought that past *me* you could sneak
This orgy between squash and leek?
Well I think *not!"* the tot then roared,
Brandishing his knife-like sword.
"Oh Mother! Why? How could you risk it?
You let my pudding touch my biscuit!"
There followed swordplay of the like
Not often seen twixt Mum and tyke.
If Mister Picky thrust and lunged,
Mother parried, flicked and flunged.
But usually, in armed combat,
Mum would get him on the mat.
Then as he'd been in Mother's womb –
A hostage in a padded room –
She'd lock him up with help from Father,
But oh the fuss, the noise, the bother!
Without misgivings or regrets,
He'd utter heartless, vicious threats.

"I'll end it all one of these nights!
I'm offering myself last rites!
Alas, I die! My heart grows still –
I'm making out my final will!
I'm phoning all the TV stations,
Armies and United Nations!
I swear I'll do it, just you wait
I'll shatter every cup and plate!
I'll smash the pots and frying pan!
I'll call the cops!
I'm calling Gran!"
So mealtimes ended in a flap,
Because he was the sort of chap
To threaten matricide if Mother
Put one food atop another.
And once he'd broken Father's legs
Because his creamed corn touched his eggs.

One suppertime not long ago –
Suspenseful, tense, and very slow –
His parents watched and barely moved,
Until the meal had been approved.
Until their son had duly made
A pickled sausage barricade,
And built a pretzel chainlink fence,
Ditches, moats, ramparts immense,
Until his plate had on its edge,
A massive mashed potato hedge,

They held their breath, afraid his food
Would intersect, and be pooh-poohed.
But all was well – a peaceful scene
With Mister Picky calm, serene,
As he took both fork and grape,
And so the fruit could not escape,
He skewered it upon a spike –
Like a head atop a pike –
And in the manner of dictators,
(As a warning to all traitors),
Staged a head-on-pike parade,
And any food that disobeyed,
Would know it better stay in line,
Or end up oozing on a tine.
Thus were his parents optimistic
That he wouldn't go ballistic.
They gazed at their despotic child –
Mother grinned and Father smiled –
They let themselves relax, unwind,
And revel in that peace of mind,
That only comes when folks can say,
"Our son's killed no one yet – today."
And like a wave the tension broke,
As Father told a knock-knock joke,
And Mister Picky screamed with joy,
And Father hugged his little boy,
And Mother – dreaming of a daughter –
Poured her son a cup of water.

Fast-forward just five minutes more,
You'd think all would be as before,
With Father looking on, adoring,
And Mister Picky's laughter, roaring,
And Mother, trying to get him fed,
With happy face and throbbing head.
And everything *was* grand until,
The tot grew hushed and very still,
And reaching for his drink – alas –
The boy looked deep into his glass.
"What's *this?*" he cried with trepidation,
"What is *this* abomination?
My eyes! My eyes! Do they deceive?
And seeing do I dare believe?"
His eyes formed odd, concentric rings,
They bulged right out, as if on springs,
He cried, "Dear God!" He shouted, "*No!*"
For what he saw was . . .

$$H_2O!$$

"Help!" he yelled, his senses tingling,
"My H's and my O's are mingling!"
"What?" his father said, "Oh, please!
You can't see particles like these!
Now you've gone right off the rails!
They're *elements*, not blasted whales!"
The tot jumped up, incensed, upset,
And brandishing a long baguette
He cried, "I do defy you, Sir!"

He turned to Mum, "And also her!
For tell me *this,* if this you know:
Is water made of H and O?"
"Um . . ." said Dad – "Ha!" cried the chap,
"You fell into my little trap!
You *know* the hydrogen's bound up
With oxygen inside my cup!
Admit they touch, you scurvy scum!"
And yelled whilst 'rounding on his mum,
"Confess – or *die,* and pay your debt –
Disembowelled by baguette!
En garde, foul wench!" he screamed and leapt,
But Mother, who was lithe, adept,
Caught her offspring in midair,
And though he screeched, "It isn't fair!
Unhand me, tart, and face my bread!"
She dragged him, kicking, off to bed,
Whence he had a raging pout –
Shut in the brig for a time-out.

Next morning peace reigned in the house,
As Mum sipped coffee with her spouse,
In front of them the table set,
With jam and toast and squashed baguette.
And Father ate unhurriedly,
In jolly, jammy luxury,
And when he'd stretched and had a yawn,
He asked, at last, "Where's Genghis Khan?"

And Mum replied, "This is the most,
Wonderfully delicious toast!"
"Too true, too true," said Father, "but
We'd better get the little mutt."
Mother's answer was to shrug,
And pour some coffee in her mug.
"On second thought," Dad said, "You go.
You gave birth to him, you know.
Just send me back a full report,
I'll read the paper – hold the fort."
And Father disappeared to muse,
Behind a copy of the news.
"Lovely," Mother said, and went,
But "lovely" wasn't what she meant.
Her twitching eyelid was a sign
Her good cheer wasn't genuine.
The way she walked with martyred tread,
The way her eyes rolled in her head,
The way she moaned and screamed a lot,
Suggested happy she was not.
Yet when she had a violent twinge,
And ripped her son's door off its hinge,
Heaving it to kingdom come,
Maternally – like King Kong's mum –
Her fit of temper seemed to soar
Out the window with the door.
A monsoon of fresh mother's love,
Sent from (where else?) heav'n above,

Flowed like syrup – viscous, sweet,
Enveloping, like warm concrete.
She flew, an angel without wings,
Held in the air by apron strings,
And landed at her dear son's knee –
"Your love," he coughed, *"It's choking me . . ."*
To which his mother said, "Dear, dear,
Don't worry, Precious, Mummy's here.
Now did she hear a rumbly tummy?
Would Genghis care for something yummy?"
The boy leapt up, cried "Hear this now!
All sustenance I disavow!
On my word *I will not drink,*
Though I dwindle, wither, shrink;
No vapour, ice, no liquid drips,
No H_2O shall pass these lips!
Nor shall I eat, though food I crave –
I swear it on my father's grave!"
"But he's not dead!" his mother cried,
"Oh sure," the boy said, "Take *his* side."
And pouting he withdrew to bed,
And pulled the bedclothes o'er his head,
Just like a corpse wrapped in a shroud,
"I'm never coming out!" he vowed.
And – sad to say, he never did –
From Life itself the urchin hid,
Though Mother jollied, sweet and mild,
Or raged and shouted, "Wilful child!"

Though Father said, "Knock, knock! Knock, knock!"
The boy was silent as a rock.
He never said "Who's there?" again,
And Father never spoke of Dwayne,
And never said, in manner clowning,
"Dwayne the bathtub, I am dwowning!"
Never more to speak these words!
Because unlike parental birds
Who trill and sing and gently peck,
Then shove the food down baby's neck,
They couldn't make him open wide,
To get the food and drink inside.
So wrinkling like a little prune,
Deflating, like a popped balloon,
His eyes bulged out, his cheeks sank in,
His hair receded like his chin.
He lived like one caught in a drought –
Thus Mister Picky dried right out.
His mum and dad boohooed a bunch –
They couldn't laugh or eat their lunch.
But none were shocked, sad truth to tell,
When Picky died and went to hell.

II

But hell turned out to be all right
For one with such an appetite.
The drink was dull, no one had spiked it,
And that's how Mister Picky liked it.

And for the most depraved of sinners,
Hell is constant TV dinners,
Served on trays with strict divisions,
For their stodgy, bland provisions.
So mealtimes in the land below
Were lovely, with the food just so.
They even gave him special tools
To tease apart the molecules!
It wasn't sad, it wasn't grim,
Damnation rather suited him.
And oh! the people who were there,
Within the Devil's dazzling lair!
So many sinful, wicked ghosts –
Movie stars and game show hosts!
Politicians by the millions!
Older brothers by the billions!
Warriors and noble Trojans!
Scientists and theologians!
Mister Picky loved to be
In their splendid company.
They'd give him sweets, perhaps a toy,
And ask, "So who's a naughty boy?"
There was one man he liked quite well;
He'd brought a cat with him to hell,
A feisty puss who lived inside
A small steel box not two feet wide.
She was a most enchanting pet,
Upon which all would place a bet,

For when the man removed the locks,
And then you looked inside the box,
You never knew if she'd be dead,
Or quite alive and well instead.
Our young chap liked this sort of cat,
The kind that you could stroke and pat
Or fling against the wall and splatter –
When she was dead it didn't matter.
One day the imp was goading her,
This cat of Mister Schrödinger,
And so he took his cat away
And said, "Let's have a chat today.
What brings a boy like you to hell?
Brutality to cats? Do tell."
"No, it was my mum and dad,"
Responded the ungrateful lad.
"They were disgusting, vile, lewd –
They dared to serve me *touching* food.
And then there was the final blow –
They stooped to serving H_2O!"
"Excuse me?" asked the man, confuzzled,
"I'm afraid I'm rather puzzled.
Because you say you will not eat
Any foods that chance to meet,
And H_2O you will not drink,
And all because you seem to think
The elements are grasping, clutching . . ."
"Quite right!" the tyke replied, "They're *touching!*"

The kind man smiled and shook his head,
"You're quite the Sherlock Holmes," he said.
"True," replied the little lad,
"And quite the Poirot, I might add.
Hypothesize! Observe! Deduce!
Of sense and logic make full use!
The truth is then quite crystal clear,
It's elementary, Watson dear!"
The nice man laughed and gave the boy
Some jelly babies to enjoy,
And then he said, "Your case is strong –
Too bad you couldn't be more wrong."
At this the boy began to smolder,
His face grew hot, the room grew colder.
His eyes grew bright, like focussed lasers,
His gaze cut like a thousand razors.
His temper boiled, without tears,
And so the steam came out his ears.
He dropped his brows, he pinched his lips,
And put his hands upon his hips,
And said to this Schrödinger chappie,
"Mister – Picky – isn't – happy."
"A shame," the man said, "But it's true,
All that food you wouldn't chew,
The double H's and the O –
They never really touched you know."
"Lies!" the boy shrieked, brazen, strident,
Snatching up the Devil's trident,

Trying to crouch and thence to jump,
And poke Schrödinger in the rump –
A strategy that wasn't wise;
The fork, you see, was twice the size
And twice the weight of Mister Picky,
And with three tines, three times as pricky.
And so he stabbed himself instead,
Thank god he was already dead,
Because the fork pierced Picky through,
And held him fast, as pitchforks do.
"That's better," said the wise old soul,
"I'll pull the fork out, plug the hole,
After you have heard me out,
And learned what physics is about."
"Physics!" yelled the fussy tot –
As students do he screamed, "What rot!
This isn't school!" He took a swing,
The man said, "No – it's hell – same thing."
So while the rascal was constrained,
Mister Schrödinger explained:
"You see, young lad, as in a dream,
Things are not quite what they seem.
That pitchfork, say, stuck in your torso –
It's touching, surely, only more so.
Your guts, the fork, they are as one –
And yet they're really not, my son.
No atom from that three-pronged spear
Is touching you, that much is clear.

It may surprise you very much
To know that *atoms never touch!*
They can't connect, though they might try –"
"Ja, right!" said Einstein, wand'ring by.
"Except for fusion which takes place
In suns and stars way out in space,
Or in colliders where they crash,
They don't connect, conjoin, or clash."
"I don't believe you!" Picky bawled,
As on the floor of hell he sprawled.
But Mister Schrödinger went on:
"A simple power acts upon
The atoms to keep them away
From other atoms – they obey
The laws of physics that declare
They cannot touch, but they can share."
"Share what?" the boy asked curious,
The man paced 'round and answered thus:
"Electrons, Boy, and they're the source
Of e-lec-tro-magnetic force,
And that's the force that says 'By gum,
Together you shall *never* come!'"
"So what you're saying," Picky said,
Whilst from his pitchfork holes he bled,
"Is that though things may *look* attached,
There are no bits affixed or latched?
No foods can touch in ways obscene,
Because there's always space between?"

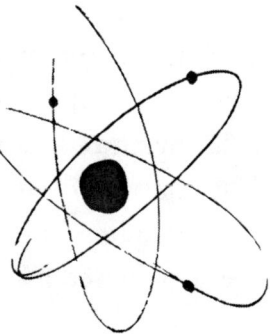

"And so much space!" the man replied,
"An atom's *empty space* inside.
It's got a nucleus it's true,
Electrons, protons, neutrons too,
But all these structures represent
A whopping total – one percent!
The rest is nothing, empty, hollow –
Does this make sense, boy? Do you follow?"
The doleful tot heard not a word,
Because to him the thought occurred
That there was so much he had missed,
Not being a trained physicist.
He wondered in the gloom and glum,
Had his death been slightly dumb?
He knew – he didn't have to guess,
The answer was a fervent *yes*.
Then Mister Picky felt a fool,
For *nothing touches*! That's the rule!
Matter's kept apart by force!
Electrostatic force, of course!
Ah! The poor boy lay as dead –
Double-dead and full of dread.
Until the man removed the spear,
And then with stealth, in manner queer,
With madness kindling his remains,
With nostrils flaring, pulsing veins,
With foaming lips, as if with rabies –
He slaughtered all his jelly babies.

III

The moral couldn't be more clear:
Be careful with the devil's spear,
Science shouldn't be ignored,
Don't use a baguette as a sword,
To fight with bread just isn't smart,
Don't call your mum a wench or tart.
In case of custard/bun infraction,
Expect complete police inaction,
And though she may be cute and frisky,
A cat kept in a box is risky.
The box is bound to get quite smelly,
And as for babies made of jelly,
Though fun to pummel, squish, and slice,
Killing babies isn't nice.
Thus ends our story of a tot,
Who was alive, and now is not.

Study Guide

1. You may have noticed that there are many barbaric words in this poem, such as mashed, tortured, oozing, kill, scum, disembowelled, slaughter, TV dinner, and – worst of all – matricide. As you may already know, matricide is made up of two parts – *matri* and *cide* – *cide* being a suffix, i.e., a little word squashed onto the rear end of another word. What you may not know is that words live in fear of accidentally sitting on a suffix, since they are like parasites, attaching themselves to other innocent words just like a leach or a tapeworm might attach itself to us. The ghastly little suffix *cide* is the most dangerous of all, however; this is because *cide* means "to kill," and what it intends to kill is the very word it is attached to! Imagine that you are a perfectly nice little word with *cide* stuck to your ending – this is like living in the same shirt and pants with someone who wants to kill you. It doesn't matter if the word is entirely innocent or has committed some terrible crime – if *cide* has snuck up behind it and grabbed hold, only tragedy can follow.

   You may remember the word "matricide" from the poem, and may now believe that this word means "to kill your mattress." This is a mistake, however, as *matri* actually means "mother," and therefore matricide means – well, I think we both know what it means and it's too awful to write about here. I shouldn't have to remind you that you should never kill your mother – unless, of course, your mother is herself a dangerous suffix (such as *phobe, itis,* or *ectomy*).

2. Did you know that the prongs of forks are called tines? Did you also know that the world's largest fork is currently located in Springfield, Missouri, and is over ten metres tall? Do you now have an urge, as I do, to go to Springfield and gaze admiringly at the world's largest fork and say, in a loud voice, "Wow! What a tine-y fork!"

3. Those readers who live in exotic places such as Norway, Belarus, Djibouti, Qatar, and Uganda may be puzzled by Mister Picky's decision to dial 911 in the case of the emergency with his bun and custard. In countries such as these, dialling 911 will not result in action by the police, fire department, or ambulance service. The most likely thing that will happen if you dial 911 is absolutely nothing, but something else might happen instead – you might, for example, get free pizza delivery, but if you were calling 911 because your house was on fire, you might not feel like eating it and it is always a shame to waste food.

Different countries have different phone numbers to call in case of emergency. For example, if you are on holiday in Italy and you need to be rescued from a mountaintop, you should dial 118, as this is the alpine rescue number. If, however, you are trapped on a mountaintop in Switzerland and you dial 118, the fire department will come instead, and if you are not on fire they will be very cross indeed and will probably spray you with their fire hoses out of spite. If you are trapped on a mountaintop in Japan and you dial 118, men in diving suits will arrive with long ropes and flotation devices because 118 is the number to call for an emergency at sea. They too will be annoyed and will likely yell harsh suggestions at you in Japanese like *"Seppuku!"* and *"Hara-kiri!"* If you take their suggestions and fall on your sword in order to ritually disembowel yourself (usually a mistake by the way), then you will need medical assistance. If you dial 118 an ambulance will eventually arrive, but it will be coming from either Indonesia or Bolivia, and thus the medical bill might be a little pricey.

Other popular emergency numbers include 000, 112, 999, and the number of your grandmother.

4. Did you know that "flunged" is a real, but sorely neglected word? Like me, do you have an urge to invent a flunger, just because it sounds like it might have comic potential? What do you think a flunger might be?
   a. An appliance for removing flippers with suction.
   b. A device for unclogging a cat.

c. Something you wear to have flunge in the sunge.

5. Like Mister Picky, are you yourself a fussy eater? Do you demand that your foods be kept strictly apart (except, of course, for foods such as ice cream, maraschino cherries, and fudge sauce)? Or are you a child who is completely unlike Mister Picky? Do you mash your foods together because you want a preview of what they'll look like in your stomach, or do you do so in an effort to avoid eternal damnation?

6. Speaking of eternal damnation, do you believe that hell is a real place, or a ridiculous, made-up place? If it is a real place, do you believe there will be physicists distributing jelly babies to children? If it is a made-up place, do you believe there will be jelly babies distributing children to physicists? Please state your reasons clearly in the form of a business letter or romance novel, and provide a 3-D origami graph with exploding pie chart.

7. Two famous people mentioned in this poem are Genghis Khan and Ervin Schrödinger. Ervin Schrödinger was a pleasant man and a scientist who invented a famous thought experiment involving a cat in a box. It must be emphasized that Mister Schrödinger *never* put a real cat in a real box, since he knew that this is a dangerous

practice and that cats are *never* to be put in boxes – except when they have to go to the vet. Then it is dangerous *not* to put a cat in a box, as they tend to want to hide in a place they think is safe which, in a car, is usually on the driver's face or under the brake pedal.

On the other hand, Genghis Khan was a largely unpleasant man and the ferocious ruler of the Mongol empire. A cat would have been lucky merely to end up in a box with him around, because Khan usually wore a yak-fur coat, but a coat made out of cats would undoubtedly have made a suitable substitute. I myself do not approve of cat-fur coats and therefore think that a much better experiment would have involved putting Genghis Khan in a box. Perhaps with a very, very, very large cat.

Cheery Bonus Section

It has come to my attention that there are many parents and teachers who feel that, considering this is a book of poetry for animals and other innocents, the overall body count is rather high, numbering as it does in the billions. Readers may remember the furor over the initial publication of this volume, when it was discovered that the average fatality rate per poem was far greater than international standards allow, and I was advised at that time to reduce the number to within legally acceptable parameters or face a hefty fine and possible jail time. In these enlightened new times, I am told, we no longer write poetry in which children are blown sky high by volcanoes as a consequence of playing handheld games, or are shot by savages just because they don't know their times table, or wind up roasting in hell for eternity just because they are picky eaters. Apparently, there were some children who burst into tears at the mention of suicidal ants who explode to protect the colony, and other children who ran from the room screaming at the image of a maniacal lizard crushing them, and all the inhabitants of the Earth, to death. In my defence, allow me to quote the immortal Piglet, after Pooh explains to him all about poetry and the proper way to write it. "Oh, I didn't know," says Piglet,* and I confess that I, too, was ignorant of modern

---

*Milne, A. A. "Tigger Comes To The Forest and Has Breakfast" from *The House at Pooh Corner*. Methuen & Co, Ltd., Great Britain, 1928.

poetry's rigorous demands.

Therefore, please find included in this volume a snappy, upbeat bonus section, in which hardly anyone gets blown up, and that concentrates on happy characters and events, such as Christmas, Easter, a visit by the postman, a visit by the Tooth Fairy, a visit by a flu virus, and the ever popular Feast of the Epiphany. Note, too, that each of the following poems can be sung, and so the musical child is advised to put on his or her liederhosen (song pants) and to sing as the spirit moves.

I hope that, this time, there will not be an international incident following the publication of *Poetry for Animals,* and that delicate, hypersensitive children will enjoy these gentle, sing-songy poems with their fusty caregivers.

Most sincerely,

I. H. Smythe

Christmas Magic

Santa has eight reindeer and
with Rudolph that makes nine,
But sadly skill at flying
is not part of their design.
Each reindeer weighs five hundred pounds,
each one's a hefty feller,
And he's not got wings or engines,
And he's not got a propeller.
Yet every Christmas eve they fly
six thousand times the speed of sound –
Does anybody know just how
these reindeer get around?
They've not got lift or thrust,
yet fly all night they must.
So how do reindeer fly?
It's simply Christmas magic!

Aye!

The mystery of Santa
makes your head gyrate and spin,
'Cause like all of his reindeer
Santa's not exactly thin.
He's got a tummy that sticks out
just like a giant egg,
And he's not enrolled at Weight Watchers
or been to Jenny Craig.
Yet every Christmas Eve he fits
Inside a space 'bout two feet wide –
Does anybody know
how such a fat guy gets inside?
He's big you must admit,
And a chimney's a tight fit.
How does he come and go?
It's simply Christmas magic!

Ho!

How does Santa find your house
within your neighbourhood?
How does he know if you are bad,
or just misunderstood?
And how come Mom burns everything,
from toast to Lucky Charms,
But Christmas dinner's always cooked
without setting off the smoke alarms?
And every Christmas eve is filled
with festive fun and mirth –
Does anybody know
how love and joy can fill the Earth?
The biggest mysteries
are things nobody sees.
Why is there peace and joy?
It's simply Christmas magic!

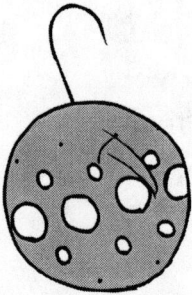

Oy!

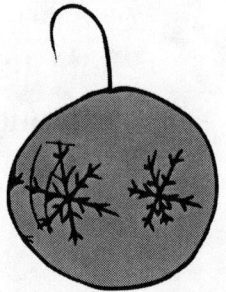

Easter Magic

The Easter Bunny hops around
the world in just one night,
And the bag of candies that he hefts
is not exactly light.
He's got a billion chocolate eggs
he made all by himself,
'Cause it's a fact that Willy Wonka's
not an Easter elf.
Yet every Easter morning
we awake to find our candy!
Does anybody know
how this here rabbit got so handy?
He does it by himself!
No reindeer, sleigh, or elf!
So how can Easter be?
It's simply Easter magic!

Whee!

Postal Magic

Like Santa Claus the friendly postman
brings stuff in his bag,
Not once a year, but *every working day*
he brings his swag!
He brings our bills and flyers,
and those packages marked *Urgent!*
And envelopes for Occupant,
and samples of detergent!
He doesn't have a reindeer
so he has to use his feet!
Does anybody know just how
he transports down our street?
He doesn't have a sled!
He goes by foot instead!
He brings our mail, but how?
It's simply Postal magic!

Wow!

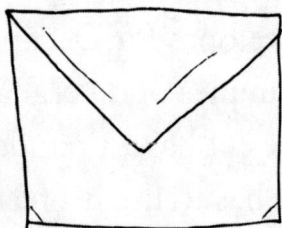

Viral Magic

Santa has ten trillion cells
that bring your toys to you,
But viruses are *single* cells
that bring you something too!
They bring a cough, they bring a sneeze
to every boy and girl,
They bring a wave of nausea
to make you belch and hurl!
And one turns into millions
in the space of only hours,
Does anybody know just how
these microbes get their powers?
A virus can't be seen,
but it can turn you green!
What brings a cold or flu?
It's simply Viral magic!

Ew!

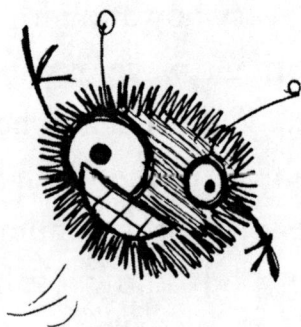

Dental Magic

The Tooth Fairy's a little gal
with some unusual traits,
She's stronger than Hulk Hogan
and she's richer than Bill Gates.
She doesn't only take a wand
and wallet on adventures –
She carries money, carries teeth,
and even Grandpa's dentures!
And every time you lose a tooth
she does a tooth and money switch.
Does anybody know just how
this Fairy got so rich?
The Tooth Fairy's petite,
but strong and rich and fleet!
She takes our teeth, but how?
It's simply dental magic!

Ow!

Epiphanic Magic

Epiphany's the time of year
when La Befana comes!
That crazy Christmas witch
who gives us treats and sweeps our crumbs.
She looks for baby Jesus
since she doesn't seem to know,
That he grew up and moved away
two thousand years ago.
And so she stuffs our socks
with all the goodies meant for him,
And in return we give her wine,
enough in which to swim.
But if you see that witch,
beware her prickly switch.
She'll clock you on the nut,
It's Epiphanic magic!

What?

Study Guide

Santa Claus, his reindeer and elves, the Easter Bunny, the Tooth Fairy, the postman and the flu virus – all of these beings are well known, but apparently there are many of you who have never heard of La Befana, or of the Feast of the Epiphany, from which the word Epiphanic is derived. Of course, if you are an Italian child, you will know all about La Befana, especially if you have actually seen her flying about on her broomstick; and if you are a Catholic child, you will know all about Epiphany, especially if your mum or your dad happens to be a nun or a priest.

If you are not Italian but you know someone who is, then you can ask that person about La Befana, and they will tell you about her ancient history, which goes all the way back to biblical times. Legend tells us that the Three Wise Men came to the house of the legendary housekeeper La Befana and invited her to come along with them to see the baby Jesus. Instead of taking them up on this once-in-a-lifetime opportunity to see the creator of the entire universe and sustainer of all Being in human form, La Befana decided that that oven of hers really needed a good scrubbing, and as for the kitchen floor, well, you don't want to know. The Wise Men continued on their journey, but even before La Befana had finished spraying on the foaming cleanser she regretted her decision and raced after the Three Wise Men. Alas, she couldn't find them, and so she searched for the baby Jesus, but she couldn't find him either. La Befana returned home, but even though the foaming cleanser had eaten right through the caramelized gunk at the bottom of her oven, she could not be consoled.

Nowadays the children of Italy know La Befana as the Christmas witch who, still looking for the baby Jesus, rides around on her broomstick, flies down their chimneys, and brings them toys and treats if they've been good, and lumps of coal or hard candy if they've been bad. It is never explained exactly *how* La Befana knows who has been good and who has been bad, but we can assume that she uses the same surveillance equipment as Santa – that is, the miniature video cameras installed by the elves in the smoke detectors on your ceiling. (You already knew about this, I trust.) It is also true that if you see La Befana she will whack you on the head with her broomstick, which strictly speaking, is illegal – but a woman who is searching for a two-thousand-year-old baby has to be cut a little slack, surely. Plus, in exchange for the candy and gifts, children and their parents leave out glasses of wine, so by the time La Befana gets to her third stop she's totally ripped, and we can only guess what she's like after her twenty millionth.

If you are not Catholic, but you know someone who is, then you can ask that person all about Epiphany and they will tell you that on that day (January 6th) they celebrate the visit of the Three Wise Men to the baby Jesus, with their gifts to him of gold, frankincense, and myrrh (although he might have preferred Hot Wheels™ and a Thomas the Tank Engine™ set, but who are we to judge). In the Greek Orthodox church, the baptism of Jesus is also commemorated. This wonderful celebration is called the Great Blessing of Waters, and to mark the occasion a priest throws a cross into the nearest body of water (an ocean, lake, or river is best, but a pool or hot tub will do in a pinch) and a bunch of enthusiastic believers then swim into the water to retrieve it. This is fun for everyone, unless the waters are shark-infested, or one of the swimmers has to wrestle the cross out of the mouth of a stray dog, or the lake is frozen solid, or someone has peed in the pool. The truly amazing thing, however, is that the water that has been blessed by the priest changes miraculously from ordinary water to incorruptible water – that is, water that can *never* go bad and will remain clear and fresh for many years. This water is called Theophany Water and it has many common, everyday uses such as keeping burglars away, improving digestion, preventing colds, and evicting demons. Clearly, if this water does what it is claimed to do, it will undoubtedly become more widely available in the near future, and I look forward to the day that bottles of Theophany Water are sold right next to the cough syrup, the burglar alarms, the digestive aids, and the wooden stakes.

Setting Traps for Santa

Each Christmas Santa visits us with reindeer, elves and sleigh,
He makes our lives a wonderland; it's magic on that day!
For we never hear the reindeer who land upon our roof,
He tumbles down the chimney, but we never hear the "Oof!"
He eats our cookies, drinks our milk,
    leaves presents 'round our tree,
Then like a thief he hoofs it in his sleigh suspiciously.
But this year will be different for Santa, deer, and elves,
We're setting traps for Santa so we'll see him for ourselves!

We're setting traps for Santa, his reindeer, and his elves,
We're setting traps for Santa so we'll see him for ourselves!

We've got nine little leg hold traps,
    they're up upon the roof,
A Texas gate at either end to catch each errant hoof,
We'll shoot each frisky reindeer with a tranquillizer gun,
And have them roped and tied before you can say "venison!"
We've dug a trench in front and back,
    a blanket o'er the trough,
And in the ditch a Rottweiler who'll bark his head right off!
If Santa makes it past the ditch, and dog, and other snares,
The tigers 'round the Christmas tree
    should catch him unawares!

We're setting traps for Santa, his reindeer, and his elves,
We're setting traps for Santa so we'll see him for ourselves!

The elves will never notice sticky glue upon the floor,
The alligator pit, the sopping sponge above the door,
Bewildered, in a daze, they'll spar and scrap
    among themselves,
O'er life-sized cardboard replicas of buxom female elves!
We've got a Venus Christmas tree, and what an appetite!
If it gets hold of Santa, then it won't let go all night!
The branches form a cradle for St. Nick to have a rest in,
But Christmas morn we'll let him go
    so that it won't digest him!

We're setting traps for Santa, his reindeer, and his elves,
We're setting traps for Santa so we'll see him for ourselves!

We've greased the chimney, hosed the steps
    so that they'll turn to ice,
We've buttered up the banister,
    the stairs we've paved with rice,
Ten thousand Lego™ pieces he will find upon the floor,
And roller skates, and toys that squeak,
    and bouncy balls galore!
There're mousetraps in the cookies,
    I wonder what he'll think,
When he finds we've slipped a Mickey Finn into his drink?

And when he trips and breaks his leg, oh what will Santa say?
"These children really love me,
   'cause they sure want me to stay!"

We're setting traps for Santa, his reindeer, and his elves,
We're setting traps for Santa so we'll see him for ourselves!

We've strung a string across the door,
   and when he trips he'll see
Upon the floor in front of him proof of our piety!
Our trophies and our badges, our report cards he'll behold,
And statements (from each other)
   that we've been as good as gold!
And though our stockings have alarms,
   we really mustn't doze,
We can't risk missing Santa, elves,
   and Rudolf's glowing nose,
The mystery of Christmas can't be solved in broad daylight,
We'll be alert upon the watch – there'll be no sleep tonight!

(But sadly both the little tykes had overlooked two things:
Though Santa may walk on the ground,
   the Sandman uses wings.
He flew around the children and he threw the sands of sleep
Into their eyes, and soon they both were snoring in a heap.)

(A tremendous shout and a mighty thump is heard –)

Wake up! Wake up! We've caught him
   and he's right here in our net,
Hooray! It worked! Now this will be
   the greatest Christmas yet!
We'll share the joy of Christmas time
   with poor old Santa Klutz,
Once we've set his broken bones,
   and bandaged up his cuts!
We lift the blanket – woe is me! – we've only caught our dad,
The dog is chewing on his leg, he seems a little mad.
All our schemes have been for naught!
   Oh Father, what went wrong?
Oh what is Daddy saying?
   "Zargle fargle ding dang dong!"

We set our traps for Santa, but we missed again we fear,
I guess he's had some practice from the traps we set last year.
We won't give up! We'll try again, and bet you even money,
We'll catch our Guardian Angel, Tooth Fairy, and Easter
   Bunny!

We're setting traps for Santa, his reindeer, and his elves,
And next year – *guaranteed* – we'll finally see them for
   ourselves!

Acknowledgments

A million thanks to Sappho and Rigel who provided many of the ideas and the inspiration for the poems in *Poetry for Animals*. It was Rigel, for instance, who dreamt up the idea of Laserhosen, and who, among many other things, brainstormed with me for newspaper headlines to use in "The Lizard." Sappho and Rigel both gleefully came up with the ideas for ambushing Santa for the poem "Setting Traps for Santa," and I couldn't have asked for more ingenious, or more demented, creative consultants. Special thanks and money to Sappho for the charming illustrations. Thanks also to Mom and Dad, who fondly remember me writing poetry on my cell walls while I was still a blastocyst. And a novemquinquagintillion thanks to Steve, for everything, but especially for letting me shamelessly pilfer so many of his great ideas and use them for my own ends.

9 781462 001996